David Lynn and Mike Yaconelli

**ZONDERVAN PUBLISHING HOUSE**
Grand Rapids, Michigan

Tension Getters Two

Youth Specialties books published by the Zondervan Publishing House
1415 Lake Drive, S.E., Grand Rapids, Michigan 49506

Copyright © 1985 by The Zondervan Corporation
Grand Rapids, Michigan

**Library of Congress Cataloging in Publication Data**

Main entry under title:

Tension getters.

Vol. 2 by Dave Lynn and Mike Yaconelli.
Includes index.
Summary: Strategies for dealing with problems and making decisions in a moral way.
1. Youth—Conduct of life.   2. Youth—Religious life.
[1. Christian life. 2. Decision making. 3. Ethics.]
I. Lynn, Dave.  II. Yaconelli, Mike.  III. Rice, Wayne.
BJ1661.T46  1984        241        84-13084
ISBN 0-310-45241-4 (v. 1)
ISBN 0-310-34931-1 (v. 2)

All rights reserved. No part of this publication may be reproduced, stored in a retrieval system, or transmitted in any form or by any means—electronic, mechanical, photocopy, recording, or any other—except for brief quotations in printed reviews, without the prior permission of the publisher.

*Edited by Marilyn McAuley*
*Designed by Ann Cherryman*

*Printed in the United States of America*

88   89   90   91   92   93   94 / AK / 13   12   11   10   9   8   7

OTHER YOUTH SPECIALTIES BOOKS

*Called to Care*
*Creative Socials and Special Events*
*Far-Out Ideas for Youth Groups*
*Good Clean Fun*
*Great Ideas for Small Youth Groups*
*Greatest Skits on Earth*
*Greatest Skits on Earth, Volume 2*
*High School Ministry*
*High School TalkSheets*
*Holiday Ideas for Youth Groups*
*Hot Talks*
*Ideas for Social Action*
*Incredible Ideas for Youth Groups*
*Intensive Care*
*Junior High Ministry*
*Junior High TalkSheets*
*Organizing Your Youth Ministry*
*Play It! Great Games for Groups*
*Super Ideas for Youth Groups*
*Tension Getters*
*Tension Getters II*
*Unsung Heroes: How to Recruit and Train Volunteers*
*Youth Specialties Clip Art Book*
*Youth Specialties Clip Art Book, Volume Two*

# CONTENTS

*Situations that help your youth group deal with the tension between what one would do, what one should do, and what Jesus might do.*

*Your youth group is asked to provide responses to situations to which there are no easy answers.*

*The Tension Getters in this section call upon your youth group to decide what they would do, and why, as different characters in various situations.*

*This set of Tension Getters challenges your group to identify problems or concerns and then determine an acceptable response.*

*The Tension Getters in this section require your group to rank each character in a story and to provide reasons for the rankings. You may also decide to add further discussion questions of your own.*

# INDEX BY TOPIC

# INTRODUCTION

Today's youth live in a complex and rapidly changing society. Moral standards that once seemed written in stone are now disintegrating. There seems to be no set of agreed-upon standards and values. As a result, young people are set adrift in a bewildering sea of moral choices without the aid of a moral compass. They are faced daily with an ever-increasing number of options and alternatives without the assistance of a moral map.

In past generations, society agreed upon a widely held set of values. Society rewarded those who went along and penalized those who did not. The cultural norms, more often than not, coincided with biblical norms. Not any longer. Now, young people are being taught that the only norm they can depend on is themselves. "Whatever is right for you" has become the only moral absolute. The result is that moral certainty has been replaced by moral confusion, and the issue in the church has become, "How can we help young people make moral choices in a world that presents so many options?" We are faced with the difficult task of preparing our young people to make right decisions in a culture that no longer cares what is right or wrong.

To put the dilemma of the church in practical terms, we must decide how the church is to deal with the issues of the present in the artificial environment of the Sunday-school room where options seem black and white. As soon as our young people move out of the classroom, they are faced with complex choices that are neither black nor white. They leave the world of simple solutions and enter the real world of not-so-simple solutions.

Stated simply, the problem is one of transfer. The church needs to provide a learning environment where young people can take what they learn in the classroom and apply it to the world outside the classroom. If they cannot transfer what they learn, then it won't be long until they become frustrated and decide to abandon their faith because it does not seem relevant to life. That is why we have published **Tension Getters.**

**Tension Getters** is a book of strategies designed specifically to help your young people transfer what they have learned in the classroom to daily life. Each strategy has been chosen for its close resemblance to real-life situations and issues. We hope that when your young people encounter similar situations in the real world, they can transfer the knowledge and skills acquired while using these strategies. Helping young people be prepared for decisions in the real world is the function of **Tension Getters.** Here's how it works:

1. **Tension Getters** creates tension.

Each strategy in this book has been included because of its potential to create a dilemma or situation with conflicting issues that require young people to think through all possible alternatives and consequences before arriving at a moral decision. Tension is created when there is an overlap of values that make a simple black-and-white response impossible. Most decisions in the real world require sifting through layers of values before a choice is made. For example, let's suppose a young person is asked to help a friend cheat on a test. The student is torn between friendship with the friend, friendship with the other students, the personal value of honesty, and so on. A diagram would look like this:

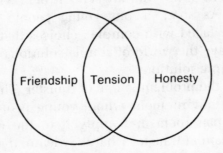

Where these values overlap is the area of tension. A decision must be made in the midst of the reality that all of these values are present at the same time. The issue becomes one of deciding which value has priority in the presence of all other values, rather than deciding which one is right or which one is wrong. Recreating this tension helps a young person think through their value system and become conscious of its implications in real-life situations.

2. **Tension Getters** requires an atmosphere of growth.

One of the biggest obstacles to overcome with young people in the church is their preconceived idea that church is where you learn all the right answers. Because we believe the Christian faith is the ultimate answer to the problems of life, young people misunderstand this to mean that it provides a specific answer to each particular problem in life. The Christian faith does provide a foundation upon which young people can deal with the particulars of life, but they must learn how to decide on those particulars themselves. For that reason, **Tension Getters** does not provide answers; it creates questions—the kinds of healthy questions that cause growth.

For growth to occur, it must happen in an atmosphere of neutral openness. That does not mean the leader or the church is neutral on any one issue; it simply means that the leader allows the freedom for all points of view to be expressed without judgment. It is important to make the young person feel that what matters more than the *right* answer is *their* answer. Here's how to create this kind of atmosphere:

1. Open-ended discussion

It is most important not to push or force the group's discussion to a conclusion. Certainly the group should stay on the subject, but you do not need to resolve all the loose ends in forty-five minutes. Discussion is squelched when young people feel pressure to end on time and to resolve all issues. The emphasis ought to be on arriving at as many options as possible so that when the decision is made, it is made with all of the alternatives in mind.

## 2. Freedom to say what one thinks

Young people are often penalized if they say what they really think, especially if what they say is diametrically opposed to what the church or the leader thinks. This makes them reluctant to express their real feelings, so it is important to affirm legitimate expressions of opinion no matter what the content. Remember, because you allow young people to say what they believe does not mean that you agree or approve of their ideas. It simply means that you approve of their right to express their ideas and enter them into the arena of discussion.

The best response to any comment is to show interest and ask for more. Probe them in a nonthreatening manner and ask them to explain why they believe the way they do. Push them to follow their idea to its logical consequence, and then let their ideas sink or swim on their own merits. If you feel it is necessary to respond to their ideas, you can always refer to it later when giving your concluding remarks.

## 3. Recreating the realities of life

Three ingredients have to be present in a discussion if you are to simulate a real-life situation:

### A. Situations involving real people

It is much easier for a young person to defend "Tom" than it is to defend their own personal belief system. They do not feel threatened when discussing other people's beliefs, but the fact is that when they talk about the Tom in the story, they are really telling you what they believe. Through a story about someone else, they are actually expressing their own value system.

### B. Complex Characters

The characters in **Tension Getters** have good qualities and bad qualities. There is enough of a mix of good and bad, just like in real life, to make a simplistic response impossible. It is easy to decide who is right when someone is all good like the Lone Ranger, but all people are a mixture of good and bad, and the strategies in the book are full of ordinary people like that.

## C. Mixture of consequences

**Tension Getters** are constructed in such a way that whatever decisions are made, they have both good and bad consequences; they help one person while hurting another, and the young person must decide on the basis of who gets hurt the least.

# HOW TO USE TENSION GETTERS

**Tension Getters** is participant centered rather than leader centered. If you want to use these strategies successfully, all members of the group need to be encouraged to participate. You must foster a climate that is conducive to discussion by communicating that each person's opinion is worthwhile and that each person has a responsibility within the group to contribute to the solution(s). For these strategies to have any meaning, there must be a variety of opinions and viewpoints.

## Starting The Discussion

Pass out to each person a copy of the strategy to be discussed along with a pencil and extra paper for note taking. Instruct the group that the strategy given is the total story. They cannot add, subtract, or ask "what if" questions. They are to deal with the story as it is. Once everyone has read the story, you can then divide them into small groups of five to seven (unless your youth group is already a small group). Have each group assign a facilitator* to keep the discussion moving and a recorder to keep a record of the decisions made so they can be reviewed or reported to the larger group. The facilitator then starts the group going by asking the assigned questions. The group then discusses the questions and attempts to arrive at one or more conclusions. If a group appears to be stymied, you may want to get them back on the track by throwing out some new ideas, playing the devil's advocate, or attempting to summarize what has already been discussed.

## Ending the Discussion

Once the discussion has reached a point where all the options have been explored, it is time to make some decisions. If you have more than

---

*The facilitator should be one of the young people. If, however, you have several adult youth leaders, you may wish to have each one assigned to a different group. Make sure each leader becomes an equal member of the group. They should not dominate the group, and if the group looks to the leader for "the answer," have the leader direct the question back to the group.

one group, then each group should arrive at a consensus (if the group cannot arrive at one consensus, they should compile minority reports). Allow all views to be shared and open it up for a group discussion of the topic. This is the time when the youth leader can provide some definite structure to the discussion. The leader may want to leave the topic hanging until the following week and encourage the young people to talk to their parents or others. This gives the young people time to digest all the implications of the issues raised during the discussion. You may want to complicate the discussion by adding new information to the story such as, "What if Tom were a Christian?" or "What if Linda only had six months to live?" You might decide that such a complication needs to be added to meet the specific needs of your group. There may be times when you want to summarize the discussion and use it as a springboard for a teaching opportunity. Finally, you can allow the questions raised during the discussion to go unanswered, allowing the youth group to wrestle with the issue(s) on their own.

## Using Scripture

Each of the strategies in this book is followed by Bible references. These references were selected for their relevance to the particular strategy and for their potential to generate healthy discussion and to stimulate dialogue. They are not to be considered exhaustive. Sometimes obvious passages that could apply have not been listed. We have assumed that you will feel free to add whatever Scriptures you believe are equally relevant. None of the Scriptures listed are intended to provide "the answer" to the ethical dilemma you are discussing. Instead they are there to shed light on the situation and give practical guidance by focusing on the question "What does God say about this?" It is important not to abuse the Bible by using any of these passages out of context, but it is also important not to deal with the difficult decisions in life without the input of Scripture. The passages listed are just the tip of the iceberg, inviting you to "search the Scriptures" and dig deeper.

Here are some suggestions that we believe will help you use the Scripture references effectively:

1. Read the Scriptures out loud together. It is important for the group to focus on the Scriptures together so all the members can deal with the biblical implications for the strategy being discussed.

2. Take the Scriptures separately and check the context to see what effect it has on the meaning. See if the group can come to an agreement on the meaning of the passage, and then apply the meaning(s) to the strategy you are discussing. Does it have any relevance? How does it affect your decision?

3. Take all the Scriptures together and see if the group can summarize the relationship of the passages. For example, after reading a number of passages relating to adultery, the group's summary statement might be "although God is against adultery, He also seems to treat the adulterer with love." Apply your summary statement to the strategy you are discussing. How does it affect your decision?

   Be prepared for the fact that some Scriptures will actually make the decision-making process more difficult. There are many Scriptures that seem to present opposing viewpoints on the same issue. Whether that is true or not, we have not used Scripture as a gimmick. We have tried to honestly present relevant Scriptures (whether they speak clearly or vaguely) with the knowledge that "all Scripture is profitable," and that God's word will not return to Him void.

# WHEN TO USE TENSION GETTERS

**Tension Getters** is not a curriculum. It is not designed to be used every week. Each strategy is different and can stand on its own. The strategies in this book are best used in conjunction with other material. **Tension Getters** is not a book full of gimmicks or quickie programs that will keep your young people busy for an hour. They are supplemental and are most effective when used as part of a larger unit. These strategies can meet a variety of needs if used properly.

## Discussion Starters

A primary function of **Tension Getters** is to create lively discussion. Each strategy is a story and almost all of them relate to situations similar to those your young people encounter every day. As a result, you can count on the interest level being high. In other words, rather than beginning your youth meeting with "What do you think about cheating?" you can start with a story about Tom, the school jock, who asks a friend to help with an upcoming test. Everyone in your youth group will have an opinion about what should be done.

## Spiritual Thermometer

As you observe the discussion generated by **Tension Getters,** you can discover, in a nonthreatening atmosphere, what your young people believe. By taking in the entire process of decision making, you can know not only what the kids in your youth group believe but how they got there. This is invaluable for the youth leader who wants to know his or her students and understand what their needs are. If the content of your program is based on the needs of your youth, **Tension Getters** should become an integral part of your program.

These strategies are also effective in helping your young people discover what they really believe. "The Island Affair" (number 103 in the first volume of **Tension Getters**) was used at a young-adult conference a few years back. Before the strategy was used, the conferees were asked if they believed in situational ethics. Not one person admitted that he or she did. After the strategy (which involves the issues of situation ethics), over fifty percent of the conference realized that they did believe in situational ethics, at least in this instance. This knowledge was not only invaluable for the conferees themselves, but also for the leaders who could then focus on that particular issue.

## Creative Alternatives

Although **Tension Getters** is full of strategies that are great discussion starters, there are many other possibilities. You can use these strategies to introduce a role play, to stimulate some creative writing, or to set the scene for a skit or dramatic situation. The possibilities are endless once kids are motivated.

You will find one other advantage to these strategies: They create tangent issues. Because these strategies deal with many different values at the same time, you will often find your young people talking about something that has nothing to do with the main topic. In the process of the discussion, they have focused on a tangent issue. Sometimes, you will want to get them back to the main topic, but often you will want to pursue the tangent issue because it expresses a need you weren't aware of.

# CAUTION

Remember that you are the final authority when it comes to programming for your youth group. You are the one who must decide whether or not your group needs more tension at this time, whether they are mature enough to hear all the alternatives, and whether they are spiritually able to deal with conflict. Here are some guidelines you ought to keep in mind:

1. Know your kids well. Some young people are not ready to handle certain problems. You might have planned to discuss the issue of death, but because one of your young people has a parent who is dying, it may not be the time to discuss that subject. It might also be the perfect time, but only you can make that decision if you know your kids well.

2. Do not dump on kids. There are many issues of our faith that are difficult for even adults to handle. Be careful not to shoot holes through all of their arguments just to create conflict. As young people mature, they not only learn more, but they learn to handle more ambiguity. Make sure your young people are getting a lot of positive content along with content that creates tension.

3. Do not try to shock kids for effect. If you play the devil's advocate, make sure your arguments are sensible. In other words, don't become so artificial in your role as spoiler that the kids don't take your point of view seriously. Sometimes leaders try to shock kids with extreme arguments or positions that, more often than not, have a reverse effect. The kids treat the discussion more like a skit and the discussion degenerates into a meaningless exchange.

4. Give people time. Don't feel like every issue must be resolved in sixty minutes. Let the young people go home thinking. Let issues stay unresolved for a while. It takes time to think through issues, and when

young people are carrying unresolved issues, they usually end up talking with someone about them ... like their parents or friends ... and that kind of dialogue can be very productive.

5. Don't be afraid of controversy or failure. When you create tension, deal with controversial issues, send people home with issues unresolved, or disturb beliefs that people are comfortable with, you are going to generate criticism from young people as well as from parents. Sometimes the criticism will be justified; sometimes you will make mistakes; and sometimes you may even lose a young person, but those are the risks of good education. Admit your mistakes, learn from your failures, but don't back off simply because you have pushed people into new areas of growth and maturity.

We think you will find **Tension Getters** an invaluable resource. Enjoy it. Use it wisely, selectively, and prayerfully. We hope you will find this book to be a significant contribution to your youth group's spiritual growth and development.

# SECTION ONE

# WHAT WOULD JESUS DO?

# 1 ■ THE DISAPPEARING FAILURE NOTICE

Julie rushed home. *Good,* she thought, *I beat Mom to the mailbox.* Midterm progress reports were out. The failure notice in geometry would definitely not be a big hit. Since the divorce, Julie's mother had been bugging her to improve her grades. Julie had tried, but Mr. Bradshaw didn't teach geometry very well.

Julie vowed to improve her grades. She knew she could do better. Why upset her mom when the quarter grades don't count anyway?

▶ What would you do in Julie's situation? Reason?

▶ What should you do in Julie's situation? Reason?

▶ What would Jesus do in Julie's situation? Reason?

 Scripture Guide:   Genesis 12:11–13   Proverbs 20:17
                   2 Kings 6:19–23    Jeremiah 17:9
                   Psalm 35:20

# 2 ■ CAUGHT IN THE MIDDLE

Ann cornered Patti in the hall. "Patti, have you heard about Barb and Mike? They have been . . . well . . . you know. Can you believe it?"

Patti hesitated. All four went to the same church, and Barb was a pretty good friend of Patti's. She thought, *I have been wondering about them. It's probably true. He did it with me when we went steady . . . the louse!*

Should Patti tell Ann she doesn't like her big mouth? Should she tell Barb the word's out? Should she confront Mike or keep quiet?

▶ What would you do in Patti's situation? Reason?

▶ What should you do in Patti's situation? Reason?

▶ What would Jesus do in Patti's situation? Reason?

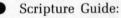 Scripture Guide:   Leviticus 19:16      2 Thessalonians 3:11−13
                    Proverbs 16:28       1 Timothy 5:13

# 3 ■ THE STEPFATHER DILEMMA

Denise has decided to run away. Her home life is horrible, and it's getting worse. She hates her stepfather. Actually, she's afraid of him. More than once he has made sexual advances toward her. Denise is afraid to tell anyone about her fears. She doubts that her mother would believe her. If her mother *did* believe her, it could lead to another divorce. One divorce is enough for anyone to have to experience. Denise doesn't want anyone to know—not Kevin (her boyfriend) or her mother or anyone. Maybe it's her fault that her stepfather acts the way he does. Denise asks Kevin to loan her some money so she can go to live with her father in another state.

▶ What would you do if you were Denise? Reason?

▶ What would you do if you were Kevin? Reason?

▶ What should Denise do? Reason?

▶ What would Jesus do in Denise's situation?

 Scripture Guide:    Psalm 27:10          Ephesians 5:11
                    Isaiah 41:10         Ephesians 6:4
                    Ephesians 4:31–32

# 4 ■ WHY ME?

Melinda was crying because her poem was selected by the English teacher to be printed in the school yearbook. *Why do things like this always happen to me?* she thought. All she had done was copy a poem out of her father's book of poetry. Never in a million years did she think something like this would happen. She was sure her father would recognize the poem.

▶ What would you do in Melinda's situation? Reason?

▶ What should you do in Melinda's situation? Reason?

▶ What would Jesus do in Melinda's situation? Reason?

● Scripture Guide:   Exodus 20:15        Galatians 6:7
                     Numbers 32:23       Ephesians 4:25
                     Ecclesiastes 12:14

# 5 ■ STRETCHING THE TRUTH

Kim's parents believed her again when she told them she didn't know she was an hour late. They trusted her. Kim didn't think it was her fault that she had to stretch the truth so often. She believed she wouldn't have to do it at all if her parents weren't so strict. Her curfew was just too early. All of her friends were allowed to stay out much later. Kim had tried talking to her parents several times, but they didn't seem to listen.

▶ What would you do in Kim's situation? Reason?

▶ What should you do in Kim's situation? Reason?

▶ What would Jesus do in Kim's situation? Reason?

 Scripture Guide:　　Psalm 35:20　　　Romans 7:11
　　　　　　　　　　　　Proverbs 23:25　　Romans 7:18–23
　　　　　　　　　　　　Proverbs 30:11　　Colossians 3:20

# 6 ■ WHAT HE DOESN'T KNOW WON'T HURT HIM

"Mom, if Jeff calls, please tell him I'm out with Tracy." Michelle wants her mother to cover for her while she goes out with Brad. Michelle doesn't want to lose Jeff, and if he knew she was going out with someone else, . . . well, no telling what would happen. She rushes out of the house before her mother has a chance to respond.

▶ What would you do in Michelle's mother's situation? Reason?

▶ What should you do in Michelle's mother's situation? Reason?

▶ What would Jesus do in Michelle's mother's situation? Reason?

 Scripture Guide:  Leviticus 19:3         Proverbs 29:15
Psalm 15:1−2         Isaiah 33:15−16
Psalm 120:2−3

# 7 ■ NO BIG DEAL

Andy ditched his first-period government class to go out to breakfast with his girl friend. It was a boring class anyway. A substitute teacher was showing a film he had already seen in another class last year. The student aide promised to mark him present. No harm done. Besides, everybody did it. Andy had ditched lots of classes all through high school, and he still had a 3.8 average.

The government teacher saw Andy and his girl friend leaving the campus and decided to give Andy's mother a call. That evening his mother asked him how his government class was that day.

▶ What would you do in Andy's situation? Reason?

▶ What should you do in Andy's situation? Reason?

▶ What would Jesus do in Andy's situation? Reason?

 Scripture Guide:     Proverbs 14:12; 20:11     1 Corinthians 10:13
                               Romans 12:21              Hebrews 13:18

# 8 ■ BILL AND JACK DANIELS

Bill's locker is next to DeWayne's. One day DeWayne accidentally saw a bottle of Jack Daniels whiskey tucked under a sweater in Bill's locker. DeWayne said hello to Bill, even though they were not good friends anymore. There was no reply. DeWayne knew all about Bill's drinking. Everyone did. Bill needed help.

DeWayne wasn't sure what had happened. They used to work on the church youth council together. Until a year ago, Bill had attended church with his parents. Now they seemed to have given up on him. DeWayne thought about telling the school counselor, but ratting on him didn't seem like such a great idea.

▶ What would you do in DeWayne's situation? Reason?

▶ What should you do in DeWayne's situation? Reason?

▶ What would Jesus do in DeWayne's situation? Reason?

 Scripture Guide:     Genesis 4:9          1 Corinthians 12:25
                                          Jonah 4:11           Galatians 6:1
                                          Acts 20:35

# 9 ■ DID SHE OR DIDN'T SHE?

Sharon broke up with Ron last weekend because he was pushing her to have sex. However, the word around school is that Sharon is pregnant. Sharon didn't have sex with Ron and is devastated by all the rumors. Apparently, Ron had been telling all his friends that he and Sharon were doing it frequently. Sharon doesn't know what to do.

▶ What would you do in Sharon's situation? Reason?

▶ What should you do in Sharon's situation? Reason?

▶ What would Jesus do in Sharon's situation? Reason?

 Scripture Guide:     Psalm 41:12          Romans 12:19
                          Proverbs 11:3        Romans 12:21

# 10 ■ SEE NO EVIL, SPEAK NO EVIL

Mark saw both boys cut the locks and steal the bikes, and the boys saw Mark. They looked like gorillas when they cornered him by his locker the next day. *Great,* Mark thought. *Now I'm going to have my face ripped off. These guys are going to kill me.* The two boys threatened Mark to keep his mouth shut or face the consequences. Mark vowed never to tell anyone what he had seen.

▶ What would you do in Mark's situation? Reason?

▶ What should you do in Mark's situation? Reason?

▶ What would Jesus do in Mark's situation? Reason?

 Scripture:            Proverbs 11:21        Proverbs 14:25
                     Proverbs 12:23        Romans 12:21

# 11 ■ TRUTH IN LENDING

Brian read, "I declare, to the best of my knowledge, that the information contained herein is true."

The statement jumped off the page at him. He had filled out his financial aid form for college, and now he needed to sign it. In his opinion, he hadn't really lied—he had only reduced the amount of money he actually had in the bank. Brian's parents both had good jobs, but they didn't make enough money to pay for Brian's college expenses. He would need all the financial help he could get.

▶ What would you do in Brian's situation? Reason?

▶ What should you do in Brian's situation? Reason?

▶ What would Jesus do in Brian's situation? Reason?

 Scripture Guide:     Proverbs 11:18        Proverbs 20:17
                     Proverbs 12:17

# 12 ■ WHO WILL LISTEN?

Sue is telling Jennifer another crude joke. Every time the girls get together, Sue has another gross joke to tell. Jennifer doesn't really like the jokes, but sometimes it's hard not to laugh—especially when everyone else does. Occasionally the jokes *are* funny. Jennifer's youth director at church says that Christians should not listen to dirty jokes. So what do you do? Tell your friends to quit telling stories, or just walk away?

▶ What would you do in Jennifer's situation? Reason?

▶ What should you do in Jennifer's situation? Reason?

▶ What would Jesus do in Jennifer's situation? Reason?

● Scripture Guide:     Psalm 1:1–2          Romans 12:1–2
                       Proverbs 13:20       Philippians 2:5

## 13 ■ READ IT OR WATCH IT

Patsie had a book report due next week. She has known about it for a month now, but as usual, she has waited until the last minute. The book has been made into a movie. It would be much easier to rent the video, watch it, and then do the book report from the movie. She still has time to read the book, but seeing the film would sure make it easier.

▶ What would you do in Patsie's situation? Reason?

▶ What should you do in Patsie's situation? Reason?

▶ What would Jesus do in Patsie's situation? Reason?

 Scripture Guide:  Proverbs 13:4  1 John 2:6
Proverbs 14:12

# 14 ■ SAVING MONEY

"Thirteen years of age and younger—$1.00 off." That's what the sign at the movies says. Clint is fourteen, but he could easily pass for thirteen. His friend Joe is fourteen too and can't understand why Clint is so paranoid about telling a little white lie. Joe says that no one will get hurt, that they can't possibly get caught, and he argues that they could use the extra dollar to buy food once they are inside.

▶ What would you do in Clint's situation? Reason?

▶ What should you do in Clint's situation? Reason?

▶ What would Jesus do in Clint's situation? Reason?

● Scripture Guide:     Proverbs 12:2          1 Corinthians 10:31
                       James 1:12—15

# 15 ■ ONE-TRACK MIND

"Hi, Linda, your sweater sure is looking good . . . uh . . . I mean, you're sure looking good." Todd and his three buddies look at each other and start laughing hysterically. Linda is angry. Every day during second period she has to put up with Todd's crude comments. His remarks always have a double meaning. Todd is a nice guy, but he seems to have only one thing on his mind.

▶ What would you do in Linda's situation? Reason?

▶ What should you do in Linda's situation? Reason?

▶ What would Jesus do in Linda's situation? Reason?

 Scripture Guide:    Proverbs 13:20      Galatians 5:16—17
Proverbs 16:30      Ephesians 5:3—4
Romans 13:14

# 16 ■ SAVING FACE OR LOSING IT

Kirk is making fun of Stan again. Kirk has been doing this to Stan since the sixth grade. This time it is over Stan's role in the school play. Kirk has been taunting Stan, implying that Stan is gay because he likes drama. Stan demands that Kirk meet him behind the gym after school. Stan has never been in a fight before, but he doesn't care. He's sick of Kirk making fun of him. He has taken all he can stand, and it's time Kirk got his. Stan waits anxiously for the end of the school day.

▶ What would you do in Stan's situation? Reason?

▶ What should you do in Stan's situation? Reason?

▶ What would Jesus do in Stan's situation? Reason?

● Scripture Guide:    2 Kings 2:23–25        Matthew 5:43–46

## 17 ■ TWO DATES IN ONE

Greg asks Jenine to be his date for the upcoming Junior-Senior Prom. She reluctantly accepts, believing it is the only offer she will get. Three days later Brian asks her to the prom. Jenine has been wanting to go out with Brian since her freshman year. She can't believe he has finally asked her. She quickly accepts, forgetting her promise to Greg. Jenine is suddenly jolted back to reality when the phone rings—it's Greg asking what color dress she is wearing to the prom.

▶ What would you do in Jenine's situation? Reason?

▶ What should you do in Jenine's situation? Reason?

▶ What would Jesus do in Jenine's situation? Reason?

● Scripture Guide:     Proverbs 11:5–6          Proverbs 21:3
                       Proverbs 12:5

# 18 ■ THE SEX TALK

Heather's mom had decided to give her "the talk." She felt that sixteen-year-old Heather was ready to hear the "facts of life." The problem was, Heather already knew everything her mother was going to tell her.

   When Heather's mom finished the lecture, she gave Heather a book to read on sex and asked if she had any questions. Heather had none. She didn't know whether she should pretend she was ignorant of the facts and ask a few questions or try and communicate her feelings about sex, or just how she should respond.

▶ What would you do in Heather's situation? Reason?

▶ What should you do in Heather's situation? Reason?

▶ What would Jesus do in Heather's situation? Reason?

● Scripture Guide:    Proverbs 15:22    Proverbs 19:8
                      Proverbs 16:23

## 19 ■ TO TELL OR NOT TO TELL

Ever since the third grade, Lori has been Kristin's best friend. Now Lori is going steady with Kristin's older brother, John. Even though John is going steady with Lori, he is also dating another girl who attends a school across town. Kristin is the only one who knows that her brother is going out behind Lori's back. And John, Kristin's brother, has asked her not to tell Lori.

▶ What would you do in Kristin's situation? Reason?

▶ What should you do in Kristin's situation? Reason?

▶ What would Jesus do in Kristin's situation? Reason?

 Scripture:          Proverbs 10:10          Proverbs 12:20
                                   Proverbs 11:13          Philippians 4:6–7

## 20 ■ GETTING EVEN

Tammie is running for a class office at school. Someone, probably her competition, is tearing down her campaign posters almost as fast as Tammie puts them up.

Cindy, Tammie's campaign manager, thinks she saw the competition ripping down one of Tammie's posters by the cafeteria. Cindy thinks tonight would be a good time to get even. She and Tammie could tear down the competition's posters.

▶ What would you do in Tammie's situation? Reason?

▶ What should you do in Tammie's situation? Reason?

▶ What would Jesus do in Tammie's situation? Reason?

● Scripture Guide:    Proverbs 29:11       Ephesians 4:26
                             Matthew 6:14–15    James 1:19
                             Romans 12:17–19

# 21 ■ A HUNGRY SITUATION

Eleven brothers and sisters, an alcoholic mother, and no father—that summarizes Roger's life. He hadn't had much of a childhood. Now, two of his sisters are in foster homes, and his older brother is in jail. His oldest sister got married and split a couple of months ago. One of his sisters has polio and can hardly walk, while another sister has a severe learning disability. Because he is the oldest boy at home, Roger feels most responsible for the welfare of the family. Last semester he quit school and got a full-time job. Two weeks ago he was laid off. There are no jobs available anywhere. He went to a church for help, but they couldn't do much. The family can't get any more welfare money, and they're out of food.

Roger is considering robbing a store or breaking into a wealthy person's house to get money for his family. He has to do something soon, and robbing seems like the only option available.

▶ What would you do in Roger's situation? Reason?

▶ What should you do in Roger's situation? Reason?

▶ What would Jesus do in Roger's situation? Reason?

 Scripture Guide:     Exodus 20:15        Proverbs 16:8
                      Proverbs 14:16      Proverbs 30:9
                      Proverbs 15:15–17   1 Timothy 5:8

# 22 ■ IT'S A LONG WALK HOME

Phil says he isn't drunk and that he can drive Troy home with no problem. Troy knows better. He saw how much Phil had to drink and thinks to himself, *I should never have come to this party.*

It is late at night. If Troy calls his parents for a ride, it may be the end of his friendship with Phil. Besides, his parents will tell Phil's parents. Since they attend the same church, Troy doesn't want that to happen. Troy considers driving Phil's car even though he doesn't have a license.

▶ What would you do in Troy's situation? Reason?

▶ What should you do in Troy's situation? Reason?

▶ What would Jesus do in Troy's situation? Reason?

 Scripture:      Proverbs 10:1       1 Corinthians 15:33
                 Proverbs 11:19

# SECTION TWO

# WHAT IF?

## 23 ■ WORKING HARD OR HARDLY WORKING

Paul had to cup his hand to hide his paper from Danny, who sat on Paul's left. Mr. Young had a vocabulary quiz each Friday, and every Friday Danny cheated from Paul's paper. Paul didn't think it was fair to have to work so hard in the class when Danny, with very little effort, received the same grades by cheating. So this week Paul hid his paper by cupping his hand. Unfortunately, Mr. Young noticed Paul behaving strangely and thought that Paul was cheating. He embarrassed Paul in front of the class by asking what was hidden in his cupped hand.

▶ What should Paul do?

▶ What if Danny were his best friend?

▶ What if Paul had cheated a couple of times himself by looking at someone else's paper?

▶ What if Danny was the first-string quarterback and needed to do well in this class to continue playing football?

● Scripture Guide:     Proverbs 12:5          1 Thessalonians 4:6
                       Proverbs 14:14

# 24 ■ THERE GOES THE NEIGHBORHOOD

The petition is plain and simple. Those signing it believe the low-income housing project should not be located in this neighborhood. Julie's father is not prejudiced, but he does worry that the "wrong" kind of people might move in and that property values will go down. He also worries that the neighborhood might become dangerous for his daughter, as well as for the rest of the family. He is leaning toward signing the petition but decides to ask Julie for her opinion.

▶ What would you say if you were Julie?

▶ What if a group home for the mentally retarded was the subject of the petition?

▶ What if a retirement home for the elderly was the subject of the petition?

▶ What if a home for troubled teenagers was the subject of the petition?

▶ What if a halfway house for paroled prisoners was the subject of the petition?

● Scripture Guide:  Leviticus 19:32     Luke 6:20–36
                    Joshua 23:11–13     Acts 17:24–29
                    Matthew 9:11        Acts 23:6

# 25 ■ ARE YOU PREJUDICED?

Kathy's father was an elementary-school principal. He had a problem and asked Kathy for her opinion. The school needed to hire a teacher. Two equally qualified people, with the proper educational credentials, had applied for the job. One applicant was a Christian; the other was not. Kathy's father was leaning in the direction of hiring the Christian, and he wondered what Kathy thought about that.

▶ What would you say if you were Kathy?

▶ What if one applicant was black, and the other white?

▶ What if one applicant was a woman, and the other a man?

▶ What if both applicants were women, but one was young and attractive, and the other was older and homely?

▶ What if one applicant was handicapped, and the other was not?

▶ What if one applicant was an atheist, and the other a Hare Krishna?

▶ What if both applicants were *not* equally qualified, and the best qualified was an atheist, and the second best was a Christian?

 Scripture Guide:    Leviticus 19:33–34      1 John 3:15
                     Galatians 3:28

# 26 ■ HE WORKS HARD FOR HIS MONEY

Craig works every Saturday doing odd jobs for people in the church. Recently, after hearing a talk in church on giving, Craig decided to give one day's wages each month to the church. He determined to start this Saturday.

After Mrs. Burt paid him, Craig stopped by the store to pick up some things for his mother. He saw a record album on sale that he had wanted for a long time. He considered using the money Mrs. Burt gave him.

▶ What would you do if you were Craig?

▶ What if Craig decided to switch weeks, buying the album this week and giving next week's money to the church instead?

▶ What if Craig's friend asked Craig to loan him some money, so that Craig couldn't buy the album or give money to the church?

▶ What if Craig's family needed the money?

● Scripture Guide:     Numbers 30:2          Proverbs 16:2
                       Proverbs 11:24–25     Matthew 5:34–37

# 27 ■ KICKING AND SCREAMING

Patti and her friends are eating lunch at the mall. A mother and her three-year-old daughter are seated at a table near them. The little girl spills her milk on purpose, giggling as she watches her mother clean up the mess with several napkins. The girls watch as the mother slaps her daughter several times. The little girl begins to cry. The mother grabs her, pulls her from her seat, and drags her out of the restaurant. The young child is kicking and screaming through the whole incident.

▶ What would you do if you were Patti?

▶ What would you do if the girl were eleven years old?

▶ What if the little girl spilled the milk by accident?

▶ What if Patti knows the little girl and the woman from church?

▶ What if, the next day, Patti sees the little girl coming out of a house down the street with two black eyes?

 Scripture Guide:    Proverbs 24:11        Ephesians 6:4
                            Matthew 19:13–15      Colossians 3:21

# 28 ■ EYE FOR AN EYE

Kimberly was angry. In elementary school, she was always made fun of because she was overweight. Remarks were never made to her face, but there were numerous times when she overheard her so-called best friends making fun of her. It didn't stop in junior high school either. Her best friends still had plenty to say behind her back.

The summer before she started high school, Kimberly stayed with her aunt in Canada. She lost thirty pounds. The change in her was unbelievable. When she started school in the fall, everyone was surprised. The plump, overweight Kimberly had suddenly become a slim, attractive long-haired blonde that all the boys wanted to be around. Now her best friends wanted her friendship, but she basically told them to get lost. She became a loner. Kimberly still had plenty of dates, but she considered all of her friends phony.

▶ What would you have done if you were Kimberly?

▶ What if Kimberly's best friends apologized?

▶ What if Kimberly's best friends began to call her stuck-up and aloof and tried to keep boys from dating her?

▶ What if Kimberly's youth director at church told her that no matter what her best friends had done to her, she had to forgive them and be friendly to them?

● Scripture Guide:    Proverbs 24:29        Romans 12:17–19
                      Matthew 10:28         2 Thessalonians 1:6–8
                      Matthew 18:21–22

# 29 ■ THE FLAT TIRE

"I can't believe it. I knew I shouldn't have done it. Why did I do this?" Steve complained to himself.

Steve's parents had loaned him their new Thunderbird to drive to the lake with his friends. He had let his girl friend drive, even though she had only received her driver's permit three weeks before. She had taken a turn a little too fast and had hit the side of the mountain. Luckily, no one was hurt, but the front of the car was demolished. A front tire blew out on impact.

Steve was in a quandary. It was bad enough that his folks' new car was wrecked, but if they knew his girl friend had been driving . . . well, . . . he didn't want to think about it. He finally decided to tell his parents that he was driving, that the tire went flat, and that he lost control of the car. It was risky, but the alternatives were a lot worse.

▶ What would you do if you were Steve?

▶ What if Steve's girl friend had been seriously injured?

▶ What if it was Steve's car?

▶ What if, after hearing Steve's story, Steve's parents decide to sue the tire manufacturer because the tire was defective?

 Scripture Guide:  Genesis 26:7         Proverbs 19:18
                  Psalm 120:2–3        Proverbs 29:6
                  Proverbs 12:17, 19, 22    Isaiah 40:28–31

# 30 ■ IT RUNS IN THE FAMILY

Dan and Stacy were seniors at North High School. They attended the same church and were leaders both at school and at church. Dan's family supported him in his school and church activities. They attended all of his functions: school plays, athletic events, and church-related activities. They were very proud of their son and his accomplishments.

Stacy's family was quite a contrast. Both of her parents were alcoholics. They refused to go to church. Stacy's father had recently lost his job. Her parents never attended any of Stacy's functions. She had the leading role in the school play, but her parents didn't come. When Stacy was crowned homecoming queen, her parents never showed up, even though they had promised they would. In spite of her family situation, Stacy excelled in all that she did.

Dan had been dating Stacy for ten months. They were planning on attending a local state college together because the cost would be easier for Stacy to handle, and this would allow them to continue their relationship. Dan had never met a girl who had so much going for her. That's why he was so blown-away when his parents informed him that they wanted him to attend a private college in another state. They said they would pay all his expenses *if* he broke up with Stacy. They pointed out that alcoholism might be hereditary and that Stacy came from a background that was questionable. Dan was furious! He couldn't believe his parents felt that way about Stacy, and he couldn't believe they would try to bribe him with the college offer.


▶ What would you do if you were Dan?

▶ What if Dan's father had two brothers who were alcoholics?

▶ What if, before Dan could make a decision, Stacy found out about his parents wishes and broke up with Dan?

▶ What if Dan had always wanted to go to a private college, but had decided it was financially impossible?

 Scripture Guide:    Deuteronomy 6:6–7    Proverbs 13:1, 13
                                  1 Samuel 3:13       Proverbs 22:6
                                  2 Chronicles 22:3

# 31 ■ A TOUGH DECISION

Helen is twenty-eight years old and the mother of four children. She has just learned that she is pregnant again. Her husband doesn't want another child, and he insists that Helen get an abortion. Helen knows they can't afford another child, but the thought of getting an abortion goes against everything she believes. She is torn between her loyalty to her husband, her responsibility for the rest of her family, and her personal belief that abortion is wrong.

▶ What would you do if you were Helen?

▶ What would you do if you were Helen and you only had one other child?

▶ What if an amniocentesis showed that the baby would be mentally retarded?

▶ What if Helen discovered that her husband was having an affair?

▶ What if Helen had fears that the pregnancy was the result of an affair she was having with another man?

 Scripture Guide:    Genesis 1:27       Psalm 139:13–15
                            Genesis 2:7        Proverbs 16:25
                            Exodus 20:13

## 32 ■ SWEET SIXTEEN

Amber tells Mr. Hartford that she is sixteen years old. It isn't quite true, but it's close enough. She will be sixteen in seven months. Amber lied because she needs the job if she is to get a car. She wished her parents could help her buy a car, the way all her friends' parents did. Mr. Hartford's company is the only one in town that is hiring teenagers, and she meets all the qualifications for the job except for her age.

▶ What would you do if you were Amber?

▶ What if Amber would be sixteen in just one month?

▶ What if Amber's father had just lost his job and the family needed Amber's money to help them survive?

 Scripture Guide:     Proverbs 11:3        Proverbs 22:3
                     Proverbs 12:19

# 33 ■ THE CONFLICT

Sandy has made a commitment to be a part of the Northside Church youth group. Sometimes the group's functions interfere with her social life—like tonight. There is a group planning meeting, but Sandy wants to go to the high-school basketball game. Her boyfriend is playing, and he gets very upset when Sandy doesn't watch him play.

▶ What would you do in Sandy's situation?

▶ What if Sandy was an elected officer of the group?

▶ What if the conflict was not a basketball game but homework?

▶ What if the conflict was a job?

▶ What if the conflict was a date?

▶ What if Sandy's brother were playing in the game?

 Scripture Guide:      Matthew 16:25       Philippians 2:3—4
                       Matthew 19:21       Hebrews 10:24—25
                       Luke 9:23

## 34 ■ NO ONE WILL EVER KNOW

Karla walks out of the store counting her change. She discovers that the cashier gave her an extra five-dollar bill by mistake. Karla can't decide whether to return the five dollars or to keep it.

▶ What would you do in Karla's situation?

▶ What if the store had shortchanged her in the past?

▶ What if the store was known for its high prices and practice of ripping customers off?

▶ What if she had been given a twenty-dollar bill instead?

▶ What if, just as Karla was getting in the car to leave, she saw the grocery checker standing outside, frantically looking around as though he had discovered his mistake.

 Scripture Guide:      Proverbs 10:2      Proverbs 15:16
                      Proverbs 14:2

# 35 ■ FORGETFUL

Sonya worked for Alex last weekend because he needed the time off to attend a church youth winter camp. He promised to work Sonya's hours the next weekend in exchange for the favor. When Alex made the promise to Sonya, he forgot that he was supposed to sing in a church musical the next Sunday. Sonya has already scheduled a trip to the lake.

▶ What would you do if you were Alex?

▶ What if Alex had forgotten he had a date with his girl friend and her parents this weekend?

▶ What if Alex had forgotten that his father wanted him to work around the house this weekend?

▶ What if Alex was coming down with the chicken pox and was very contagious?

● Scripture Guide:     Psalm 90:12        Ephesians 5:15–16
                        Proverbs 25:14

# 36 ■ SPECIAL-ORDER BABY

The Johnsons are a typical middle-class suburban white couple in their late twenties. They really want a child but are unable to have one. They tried to adopt, but they were told that they would be put on a waiting list and that it might be several years until they would be given a child. Their attorney arranges for a surrogate mother to be artificially inseminated with Mr. Johnson's sperm. She will carry the baby to full term, and once it is delivered, she will give the baby to the Johnsons. The contract is signed.

Nine months later, the baby is born to the surrogate mother, and it is severely mentally retarded.

▶ What would you do in the Johnson's situation?

▶ What would you do if you were the surrogate mother?

▶ What if the baby were perfectly normal and the surrogate mother decided to keep it?

 Scripture Guide:     Romans 14:22–23     Colossians 3:1–2
                      Philippians 2:12–16     Hebrews 11:1–31

# SECTION THREE

# HOW DO YOU FEEL?

## 37 ■ NO DIFFERENCE

Debbie dates non-Christian as well as Christian guys. Her mother doesn't like this. Debbie explains to her mom that the non-Christian guys she dates are no different than those who are Christian. (What she really wants to tell her mother is that the Christian guys are usually *worse!*) Her mother finds this very disturbing. She talks with several other parents from the church, and they also agree it would be better if Debbie dated only Christian guys.

▶ How do you feel about this situation?

▶ What is the main issue in this situation?

▶ What should be done about this situation?

 Scripture Guide:    Proverbs 13:10        Romans 7:14–25
                                  1 Corinthians 3:1–3    Ephesians 4:1–3
                                    2 Corinthians 5:17    Ephesians 6:13

# 38 ■ CONFIDENTIALITY

Dr. Morton prescribed birth-control pills at sixteen-year-old Dawn Chipman's request. After Dawn left, Dr. Morton felt guilty. She had been the Chipman's family doctor for years. She wondered if she should call Dawn's parents and inform them that she prescribed the pill for their daughter or if she should keep quiet as Dawn asked.

▶ How do you feel about the situation?

▶ What is the main issue in this situation?

▶ What should be done about this situation?

● Scripture Guide:    Proverbs 16:25      Philippians 2:12–13
                      Romans 14:19–21

## 39 ■ DRIVING WHILE INTOXICATED

Jack felt numb. His father told him this morning that his best friend, Carl, was instantly killed last night when a drunk driver hit him head-on. The driver was arrested. It's the third time he's been caught driving while intoxicated.

▶ How do you feel about this situation?

▶ What is the main issue in this situation?

▶ What should be done about this situation?

● Scripture Guide:     Job 13:15          Matthew 5:4
                       Job 14:5           Galatians 6:2
                       Psalm 146:9        Ephesians 4:26
                       Isaiah 43:2

# 40 ■ UNDER CONTROL

Occasionally, Randy smoked pot and drank a few beers at parties with his friends. He always stayed in control, and he never drove if he felt intoxicated. Randy believed he was acting responsibly and could quit pot and alcohol any time he wanted to. Many kids used drugs or drank before and after school. Randy only did it on weekends. He didn't see it as a problem. It never interfered with his school work, home life, job, or church.

▶ How do you feel about this situation?

▶ What is the main issue in this situation?

▶ What should be done about this situation?

● Scripture Guide:     Galatians 2:20          Ephesians 5:15−16
                       Romans 12:1−2           Philippians 2:5
                       Romans 8:9

# 41 ■ HUNGER HURTS

A baby died in her arms.

Seventeen-year-old Lisa had taken a trip to Haiti with her Aunt Glenda. Every year, Aunt Glenda went to Haiti to donate two weeks of her time to help the poor.

Lisa had heard about hunger and starvation, but never in her wildest imagination had she dreamed poverty could be so terrible. Lisa had never been hungry in her life, nor had she known anyone who was starving. She felt sick to her stomach as well as guilty, selfish, and angry. She felt guilty because she had so much and had never helped anyone in need before. It wasn't easy to admit she might be selfish. She was angry. It wasn't fair for these people to have so little when she had so much.

Now Lisa stood there with the lifeless baby in her arms, gone now because it didn't have enough to eat. Tears filled her eyes. She wanted to scream or run or go home and tell everyone to quit being so selfish. Lisa's confusion and helplessness overwhelmed her. Hugging the baby, she just sat down in the dirt and cried.

▶ How do you feel about this situation?

▶ What is the main issue in this situation?

▶ What should be done about this situation?

 Scripture Guide:  Deuteronomy 15:7–11    Proverbs 21:13
                   1 Samuel 2:7           Proverbs 24:30–34
                   Proverbs 19:17         Isaiah 3:13–15

# 42 ■ HOME, SWEET HOME

Jim was working at the rest home for a summer job. The conditions in the rest home were horrid. The smell was unbearable. *How can people work here, let alone live here?* Jim wondered. He was shocked by the way the elderly were treated. He didn't know what to do. The rest home had passed all the health inspections that were necessary for it to remain in operation, but something *had* to be wrong. Either someone was paid off or some health inspector was terribly negligent. Did the owners simply fix up the home whenever they knew an inspection team was coming? Whatever the reason, something had to be done. However, Jim didn't know what that something should be.

▶ How do you feel about this situation?

▶ What is the main issue in this situation?

▶ What should be done about this situation?

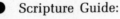 Scripture Guide:     Leviticus 19:32          James 1:27
                                1 Timothy 5:9—10

# 43 ■ THE TEASE

Jennie is such a tease—the way she walks, the clothes she wears, her language. Seduction is her middle name. She always has a date. Guys are waiting in line to take her out. The teachers at school treat her like a queen, and she always seems to get whatever she wants. None of the girls like her very much, but the guys sure do. She's a minister's daughter—one of those wild preacher's kids.

▶ How do you feel about this situation?

▶ What is the main issue in this situation?

▶ What should be done about this situation?

 Scripture Guide:    Psalm 119:44–45        1 Corinthians 8:9
                     Proverbs 20:11          1 Corinthians 9:19
                     Proverbs 21:4           1 Corinthians 10:23–24
                     Matthew 5:8             2 Corinthians 3:17
                     Ephesians 5:3–4

# 44 ■ FEELING FORGIVEN

Michelle didn't feel forgiven. She had earnestly prayed about what she had done. She was sorry and wanted to change, yet she still felt guilty because this was about the hundredth time she had asked to be forgiven. Maybe God wouldn't forgive her because apparently she didn't mean she was sorry or she wouldn't keep doing the same thing over and over. It seemed so hard to live right. Michelle began to wonder if she really was a Christian.

▶ How do you feel about this situation?

▶ What is the main issue in this situation?

▶ What should be done about this situation?

 Scripture Guide:     Psalm 103:12          Philippians 3:13—14
                     John 8:11            Hebrews 8:12
                     John 8:36

# 45 ■ WHAT'S JUSTICE?

There is no justice anymore. At least, Bill doesn't believe there is. His home was recently robbed, and a policeman was shot while trying to arrest the thief. There was a scuffle. When the policeman tried to reach for his gun, the thief's gun accidentally went off and shot the policeman. The judge dismissed the case because the policeman did not have sufficient cause to stop the alleged robber. Though he lived, the policeman will be crippled for life.

▶ How do you feel about this situation?

▶ What is the main issue in this situation?

▶ What should be done about the result?

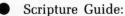 Scripture Guide:

| | |
|---|---|
| Psalm 37:28 | Romans 12:17–19 |
| Proverbs 20:22 | Titus 3:1 |
| Proverbs 24:17–18 | 1 Peter 2:13–17 |
| Proverbs 24:23 | John 7:24 |
| Isaiah 59:14 | |

# 46 ■ BOYCOTT

David Williams received a letter in the mail from a national organization asking him to boycott a certain company's products. This large multinational corporation advertizes some of its products during TV shows that have excesses of sex and violence. David considers participating in the boycott. He believes something needs to be done about the sex and violence on TV.

▶ How do you feel about this situation?

▶ What is the main issue in this situation?

▶ What should be done about this situation?

● Scripture Guide:    1 Corinthians 10:31    Philippians 2:12–16
                                2 Corinthians 10:3–5    1 John 2:15–17

# 47 ■ SEX, DRUGS, AND ROCK-'N'-ROLL

"Sex, drugs, and rock-'n'-roll. That's all today's youth think is important," Mr. Williams complains. He is seated in the teacher's lounge talking with the other teachers during break. "Most kids never study, and even if they do, they only study enough to get a grade so they can get their parents off their backs—*if* they still live with their real parents. Most kids don't know how to read or spell, and they don't care. All they care about is the weekend, getting stoned, and walking around like zombies with their cassette stereos blasting their eardrums out." Mr. Williams is wound up now.

One of the teachers looks at Mr. Williams disgustedly and says, "Then why don't you quit teaching, Williams?"

▶ How do you feel about this situation?

▶ What is the main issue in this situation?

▶ What should be done about this situation?

 Scripture Guide:    Matthew 6:33        2 Thessalonians 3:6
                    John 15:19          1 Timothy 4:12
                    Ephesians 5:11      1 John 2:15–17

## 48 ■ THERE HAS TO BE A BETTER WAY

Until his church's summer camp, Carl could not seem to motivate himself to pray or study the Bible. At camp, he made a commitment to read his Bible and pray every day. He kept that commitment for about three weeks. Now, six months later, he wondered if he was even a Christian. He hadn't read his Bible for months, and he couldn't seem to pray even though he really tried. He had gone to his youth director and was told that all he had to do was ask God to help him; then he would *want* to read his Bible and pray. But that didn't work either.

▶ How do you feel about this situation?

▶ What is the main issue in this situation?

▶ What should be done about this situation?

 Scripture Guide:   Matthew 26:41        Hebrews 4:16
                    Romans 8:26–27       James 1:5–8
                    Ephesians 6:18

## 49 ■ WHO CAN YOU TURN TO?

Julie felt so alone. She was facing a tough problem and needed advice from an adult. There was no one close to her who would listen, no one to help her with her burden. Her stomach ached. She wanted to talk to her mother, but her mother had enough to worry about with the divorce and the new job. It seemed so hard to face the problem by herself. She wished she could find someone who would care enough to listen.

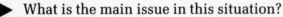 How do you feel about this situation?

▶ What is the main issue in this situation?

▶ What should be done about this situation?

● Scripture Guide:    Genesis 43:30    Romans 12:15
                      Job 2:11        Galatians 6:2
                      Matthew 26:36—45    Revelation 21:4

# 50 ■ WAITING

When Tom broke up with Chris, she thought she could never love anyone again. She had believed she was in love. It had felt like the real thing. She had been so happy.

Chris finally got over Tom, but now she's lonely. She hasn't dated for quite a while. Chris wants to date but hasn't had any offers. Her best friend keeps telling her to "wait on the Lord." That is hard to do, and Chris is tired of waiting, tired of staying home on weekends, and especially tired of being lonely. Frankly, this "waiting on the Lord" stuff sounds like a bunch of bunk.

▶ How do you feel about this situation?

▶ What is the main issue in this situation?

▶ What should be done about this situation?

● Scripture Guide:    1 Kings 19:3–14      Isaiah 46:4
                      Proverbs 18:24       Hebrews 13:5–6

# SECTION FOUR

# WHAT SHOULD BE DONE?

# 51 ■ A FRIENDLY LUNCH

The four girls were supposed to have lunch together at the mall before going shopping. Samantha had invited Carol. Samantha was also elected by Laura and Mindy to un-invite Carol. Laura and Mindy didn't like Carol. They said that Carol used to be okay until she started getting into religion. Now Laura and Mindy felt uncomfortable with Carol. Even though Carol was Samantha's friend, Samantha also felt uncomfortable with the religious stuff, so she didn't mind cancelling the lunch date. Her friendship with Laura and Mindy was more important to her than her friendship with Carol.

"Carol, this is Samantha. We decided to cancel our lunch at the mall. Mindy's parents said she couldn't go. I'll see you Sunday at church. 'Bye.'' Samantha was glad that was over.

The lunch was fun. Samantha, Laura, and Mindy really had a good time. No one even missed Carol . . . until Samantha spotted her walking toward their table. Mindy and Laura quickly excused themselves and left rather quickly. Samantha sat staring as Carol walked up.

▶ If you were Carol, what would you do? What would you say to Samantha? What would you say to Laura and Mindy?

▶ If you were Samantha what would you do? What would you say to Carol? What would you say to Laura and Mindy?

 Scripture Guide:     2 Kings 2:2        Proverbs 20:6
                                  Proverbs 18:24    John 15:13

# 52 ■ THE PLAYMATE LOCKER

Everyone seemed to like Paul. He wasn't a crude person, but his locker was full of *Playboy* magazines. He had taken them from his father's study without his dad knowing. He taped one of the centerfolds inside his locker, which became the main attraction during lunch. In fact, Paul was organizing a porno-video night next weekend when his folks were away.

Dan's locker was next to Paul's. They were sort of locker friends. Dan had never really seen much porno stuff, but as he thought about it, it sounded intriguing. Dan's folks would flip out if they knew he had ever seen a *Playboy* magazine, but Dan saw nothing wrong with looking as long as he didn't *do* anything.

Paul came up to Dan's locker. "Hey, Dan, what's happening? I've invited a bunch of my friends over this weekend for a video night. We're going to show some pretty X-rated stuff. Interested?" Dan didn't know what to say.

▶ What would you do if you were Dan? What would you say to Paul?

▶ What would you do if you were Dan's girl friend and he told you he was going to the video night? What would you say?

▶ What would you do if you were Paul's girl friend and found out about his interest in porno?

▶ What would you do if you were Paul's parents and just found out about his interest in porno?

● Scripture Guide:    Genesis 6:5        Romans 2:16
                      Proverbs 15:26     Philippians 2:5
                      Matthew 15:19

# 53 ■ DO ME A FAVOR

Jill needed the promotion. Her first year of college required a lot more money than she was making. Tuition was going up next semester. When Rick, Jill's boss, first mentioned the possibility of a promotion and a pay raise, Jill was excited. But the more Rick talked, the more Jill realized there were strings attached.

"Jill, I really think I need to know you better before I can decide whether you should get the promotion. My wife is going out of town this weekend. I wondered if you would like to come over to the house for a few drinks and dinner. I would understand, of course, if you couldn't make it, but I do need to decide on the promotion this weekend." Jill had never had anything like this happen before. She didn't know what to do.

Barbara, Jill's best friend, encouraged Jill to accept the dinner offer. She advised her to lead Rick on without yielding sexually and then, when she got the promotion, drop him.

Sandy, Jill's older sister, disagreed. She recommended that Jill go to the manager and complain of sexual harassment. Jill had thought of that but was afraid Rick would deny everything, and then she would not only lose the promotion but her present job as well. She really didn't know what to do.

▶ If you were Jill, what would you do?

▶ If you were a friend, what would you do to help Jill?

▶ If you were Jill's boyfriend, what would you do?

▶ If you were Jill's parents, what would you do?

Do you agree that Jill was being sexually harassed? If not, how would you define sexual harassment?

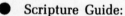 Scripture Guide:     Proverbs 8:10–21      Romans 12:12–21
                                            Proverbs 12:5           Hebrews 13:5–6
                                            Proverbs 13:20        1 John 2:15–17

## 54 ■ THE RIP-OFF

Over the past weekend, thirty-seven lockers at Benton High School were vandalized. Floyd's locker was one of them. He was furious that someone would do such a thing. Nothing was safe anymore. The school's insurance would cover the cost of the stolen items. The insurance agent asked the students to list their stolen goods, supply an accurate description of each item, and return the report to her. She did not question them about their itemized lists; she believed the students could be trusted. The principal thought she should question them thoroughly because he believed most students would pad their lists to receive more insurance money.

The principal was right. Floyd lied about a radio being stolen. Eventually he received money for the radio.

Wilma, whose locker is above Floyd's, reported truthfully that nothing of value was stolen from her locker. She knows that Floyd lied. Of course, she received no money.

▶ Does it always pay to tell the truth?

▶ Could most high-school students be trusted in a similar situation?

▶ If you were Floyd, what would you have done? If you were Wilma, what would you have done regarding Floyd?

▶ If you were the insurance agent, what would you have done?

 Scripture Guide:  Exodus 20:15      Jeremiah 2:26
                  Leviticus 6:2–7   Ephesians 4:28
                  Proverbs 22:1

# 55 ■ PARTY TIME

Owen's parents saw nothing wrong with drinking. In fact, they saw nothing wrong with Owen drinking, as long as they were with him when he drank. They felt that their presence in the room would keep their son from abusing alcohol. That's why Mrs. Karras was so upset when she unexpectedly came home early and found Owen cleaning up beer cans around the house. It was obvious that he had cut school to host an impromptu party with a group of friends. "I can't believe you would do this, Owen. You can drink anytime you want to when we are home. Wait until your father gets home. You are on restriction."

While cleaning up the mess, Owen could overhear his mother on the phone. She was calling the parents of his friends who had been at the party. His friends were going to hate him.

▶ Do you agree with Owen's parents about letting Owen drink in front of them?

▶ What did Owen do wrong, if anything?

▶ If you were one of Owen's friends, how would you feel if his mother called your parents?

▶ If you were Owen, what would you say to your mother?

▶ If you were Owen's father, what would you say and do to Owen when you got home?

● Scripture Guide:    Proverbs 20:1          Ephesians 5:18
                      1 Corinthians 6:12     1 Timothy 5:23
                      1 Corinthians 6:19–20

# 56 ■ A SCHOOL NIGHT'S SECRET MEETING

Bonnie's mother will not let her use the car for social events on school nights. If she needs to go to the library or to a meeting for church or school, the use of the car is no problem. For purely social functions, however, Bonnie's mom has made it clear that the car is off limits.

Tonight Jeff will be at a birthday party for Katrina. Bonnie has been waiting for the opportunity to meet him, and at last she will have the chance . . . except she has no way to get to Katrina's house because it is a school night. Katrina tells Bonnie that she could easily get the car by telling her mom she needs to go to the library. Bonnie agrees.

On the way to Katrina's house, Bonnie stops at the library to check out a book. She doesn't feel she is lying now, since she did go to the library.

▶ Was Bonnie's mother unreasonable?

▶ If your parents make unreasonable demands, is it okay to disobey them?

▶ Was Bonnie really lying?

▶ Did Katrina do anything wrong?

▶ If Bonnie would have asked you what she should do, how would you have replied?

● Scripture Guide:  Leviticus 19:3        Proverbs 1:8–18
                    1 Samuel 3:12–13      2 Corinthians 12:14
                    Psalm 1:1–2           Ephesians 6:1–4
                    Psalm 37:4–5

# 57 ■ A DISTURBING ISSUE

There was no telling how the Sunday-school class stumbled upon the subject of nuclear war. Ellen found herself arguing with the teacher. She believes it is time the United States took the initiative and began limiting the number of nuclear bombs it builds. She feels that there should be a nuclear freeze and that the U.S. should develop no more bombs. The teacher disagrees. She believes the communist threat must be met with a strong defense. Since the Russians are building more and more nuclear warheads, the U.S. must do the same to insure the safety of the world. She argues that the U.S. can only maintain peace through strength and that this strength prevents the Russians from involving the world in nuclear war.

James defends Ellen by arguing that the United States' strength does not lie in the number of bombs it possesses. He says that there are already too many bombs and that the strength of the nation lies in its faith in God and its strong morality.

Brad thinks the whole discussion is a joke. He feels that nothing can be done about the build-up of nuclear weapons, so there is no use trying to prevent it.

Amber, upset that the teacher and class members are discussing the nuclear issue, leaves the room. She believes the class should be discussing "spiritual things," not things like nuclear bombs.

▶ Does the nuclear issue have anything to do with Christianity and the Bible?

▶ Is there a Christian point of view, or can a Christian hold almost any viewpoint regarding the nuclear issue?

▶ How would you respond to Ellen?

▶ How would you respond to the teacher?

▶ How would you respond to James?

▶ How would you respond to Brad?

▶ How would you respond to Amber?

 Scripture Guide:     Hosea 10:13–14          Matthew 26:52
                     Matthew 5:43–48         Romans 12:18
                     Matthew 10:34           1 Timothy 2:1–4

## 58 ■ WHO'S LIFE DO YOU SUPPORT?

Steve's thoughts of Grandma Thornton are good ones. He really loves her. Steve feels lucky to have a grandmother like her.

Steve was accepted at a good Christian college. Since it was a private school and tuition was high, his grandmother said she would pay for it. But she had a stroke recently and is in a coma. The doctor says she will die, although it could be months before she does. The life-support systems that are keeping her alive are very expensive, and if Steve's grandmother remains in a coma for months, all her money will be spent on the hospital bills. As for Steve's college education . . . well, he can forget it.

Steve's father is considering asking the doctor to remove the life-support equipment and allow Steve's grandmother to die.

▶ What would you do if you were Steve's father?

▶ What would you suggest that your father do if you were Steve?

▶ What would you suggest if you were the doctor?

▶ What do you think God would want you to do?

● Scripture Guide:    Exodus 20:13          1 Corinthians 15:55−58
                      Ecclesiastes 3:1−2     Philippians 1:21−24
                      Romans 14:7−8

# 59 ■ GOD AND ROCK-'N'-ROLL

Jeff and Eric were really surprised when they came to youth group last night and heard the guest speaker discuss rock-'n'-roll. He suggested rock-'n'-roll music was from the devil. He said the words and beat were sinful and suggestive, and that many songs used "backward masking" to hide sinister messages.

Eric's parents don't like him listening to rock-'n'-roll, and they keep telling him that a Christian should listen only to Christian music.

Jeff thinks the whole thing is ridiculous. He is into hard rock and even has some records by so-called satanic groups. He believes that even though some of the words are bad, the groups just do whatever they think will make money. He believes that the groups that talk about Satan just do it to get media attention. Even though some groups see nothing wrong with drugs and may even encourage drug taking, Jeff feels he is intelligent enough to reject that kind of thinking.

▶ Which person do you most agree with: Jeff, Eric, Eric's parents, or the youth-group speaker?

▶ How would you define "Christian music?"

▶ Does God care what kind of music you listen to?

▶ Do the words in music affect you? How?

 Scripture Guide:　　Proverbs 3:7　　　　Ephesians 6:11–18
　　　　　　　　　　　　Psalm 19:14　　　　　Philippians 4:8
　　　　　　　　　　　　Ephesians 5:19　　　1 John 4:4

# 60 ■ ON THE OUTSIDE LOOKING IN

The youth group was really different—not at all like the group Ann had belonged to back home. Ann and her mother had moved when her parents divorced because Ann's mother wanted to be closer to her family for support. So here she was. It was her fourth Sunday visiting Eastside Church. A "visit," because Ann hadn't yet felt like part of the group. Her mom knew several people in the church, but Ann was getting the feeling that she would never get to know anyone. Did she have leprosy or what? The kids in the group were nothing like the kids in her old youth group. In fact, they were just as cold as the kids at her new high school.

There was Scott. He was totally interested in his girl friend. The two of them were inseparable. It was disgusting. They held hands during singing, Bible studies, games, everything! Then there was Stacy. She was either combing her hair or checking her makeup, and the games she played with the guys—unbelievable! Tom sat in the corner. People at school called him "chemical head." The church kids ignored him, but he didn't seem to care. Then there was Fred who had to tell everyone all about his weekend exploits. He partied hard and was proud of his fast life. Today he had an audience of freshmen listening to his Friday-night story. Karen . . . well, Karen always kept her nose in the Bible. She wanted a deeper Bible study, and was so involved with her Bible that she forgot about people. Today, Ann was fortunate enough to sit next to the three gossipers. Eavesdropping on their conversation was like listening to a soap opera.

Most of the people in the group acted as if they didn't want to be in church but their parents made them attend.

▶ If you were Ann, what would you do? What would you say to the rest of the group? To your mother?

▶ Is there a difference between the kids at school and the kids at youth group?

▶ How could this youth group have made Ann feel a part of it?

▶ Is there anything wrong with having a certain group of friends you enjoy being around more than others?

▶ If you are a Christian, should everyone be an equal friend?

 Scripture Guide:    Proverbs 18:24        Romans 1:12
                     Acts 2:41–47          1 John 1:7

## SECTION FIVE

# WHOM DO YOU CHOOSE?

# 61 ■ THE TWO-TIMER

Barry had been going steady with Linda for two years and was getting tired of her. She was smothering him. She always had to know where he was and who he was with. Linda was super-attractive, bright, and fun to be around. Barry knew that if they broke up, there would be a line of guys at Linda's door offering to console her. But good-looking or not, she was driving him up a wall with her possessiveness.

Don, Barry's best friend, didn't have a clue that Barry was starting to get tired of Linda. Don wouldn't have minded going with Linda himself, but as long as she was Barry's girl friend, she was off limits. Don was caught off-guard when Barry told him he had a date with another girl. "Her name is Lisa, and she is one classy girl. I think I could get serious with her," Barry said casually.

Don was angry. "But what about Linda? Are you going to break up with her?"

Barry looked surprised. "Heck no, Don, at least not for a while. I still care a lot about Linda, and I'm not sure about Lisa yet. Besides, I don't want to hurt Linda's feelings." Now Don was really upset. His best friend was two-timing Linda. It just wasn't right.

Later, Linda confronted Barry right after school. She was mad and crying at the same time. "I can't believe you would do this to me, Barry. I thought you cared about me, but then I find out you have been dating some other girl."

Barry felt panicky. For the first time in the two years they had been going together, Barry realized how much he cared about Linda. "Okay, Linda. I did go out with Lisa once, but that's all. I'm sorry. Please give me another chance."

Suddenly, Linda stopped crying and looked straight at Barry. "I wondered if you would tell me the truth. You did. So I guess I can tell you the truth. I've dated another guy a couple of times myself. I thought I was getting tired of you, but when Don told me you were cheating, I realized how much I loved you. So maybe this experience has been good for both of us."

Now it was Barry's turn to be shocked. He just stood there. He was angry at Don for betraying him and at Linda for cheating on him. He had really been a first-class sucker. He looked at Linda coldly. "Now I know who I can trust—and it isn't you or Don. Maybe you two ought to get together. You deserve each other. See you around."

When Barry arrived home, he called Don to tell him their friendship was over. Then he called Lisa to see how things were looking for the weekend.

▶ Rank the following characters from best to worst: Barry, Don, Linda, Lisa.

▶ Provide a reason for each of the rankings.

● Scripture Guide:    Proverbs 21:7          1 Corinthians 3:3
                      Matthew 6:14–15        James 5:9
                      Luke 6:31

# 62 ■ IT HAPPENED SO FAST

Jessica was just one of those girls. She was always cheerful and available when you needed her. She was active in 4-H Club, the school senate, and the drill team, and she was leader in her Young Life club. Jessica was the kind of person everyone liked. Because of her responsibilities, Jessica was busy with activities almost every night of the week.

Jessica's parents were great. They had given her the family car to use as her own. It even had a sunroof, which during the hot summers was off most of the time.

The last few days had been terrible. Jessica had to work the entire weekend at her house. Her father had taken his yearly hunting trip, so Jessica had to stay home and help her mom with cleaning before the holidays. Jessica had been up late every night during the past week, and after working the entire weekend, she was exhausted. If that wasn't bad enough, her boyfriend, Tom, called on Sunday and was mad because Jessica hadn't spent any time with him. She promised to see him Monday night. That was before she remembered that there was a Young Life leadership meeting. Rick, the Young Life director, told her that her attendance at the meeting was mandatory. Jessica decided to go, but to leave early.

At times like this, Jessica often felt like everyone was pressuring her. She was not just physically exhausted; she was emotionally drained. Just before she left for the Young Life meeting, her mother gave her a lecture about being gone too much. She told Jessica to be home before 9:00 P.M. That was okay with Jessica, because she planned to see Tom at 8:00 P.M.

Jessica arrived at the Young Life meeting on time. However, everyone else was late, so it was 7:10 before the meeting actually started. When it wasn't over by 8:00, Jessica told the group she had to leave. Rick was upset. He pointed out that Jessica's commitment was questionable if she couldn't even stay for an important meeting. Jessica stayed, but all she could think about was Tom and her parents waiting for her.

The meeting was over at 8:40. Jessica jumped in her car and headed for home. She was pushing the car by driving so fast, but she was late. As she came around Donner's Point, an animal walked in front of the car. She slammed on the brakes, and the car went out of control.

Jessica was not wearing a seat belt and was thrown from the car. Her head hit the pavement, and she was killed instantly. The police said that if she had been wearing a seat belt or had not had the sunroof off, she would have received only minor-to-moderate injuries.

▶ Who was most responsible for Jessica's death? Jessica? Tom, her boyfriend? Her parents? Rick, her Young Life director? The kids who were late to the meeting?

● Scripture Guide:    Genesis 4:9          Ephesians 5:15–16
                             Ecclesiastes 3:1–8   Philippians 1:21
                             Matthew 6:33–34    Colossians 4:5

# 63 ■ HARD CHOICES

Everything in Heather's life had been normal. She had grown up in a fine middle-class family with two brothers and a sister. After Heather graduated from high school, she completed junior college and became a legal secretary for local law firm.

Heather married her high-school sweetheart, Jerry, who was now a supermarket manager. They were active in the local church and couldn't be happier—except for one nagging problem. For the last five years of their marriage, Heather had been unable to become pregnant. According to the doctors, both Heather and Jerry were perfectly normal. There seemed to be no physiological reason for their problem.

Just as they were about to consider adopting a baby, Heather discovered, quite by accident, she was pregnant. For the past year, she had been experiencing pain in her armpit. At first she thought of the worst—cancer. She saw Dr. Hadley, the family physician, immediately. He checked her and assured her there was nothing to worry about. It was just an infection that required antibiotics.

A year passed, but the soreness never went away. In addition, Heather had begun to experience side effects from the antibiotics. She decided to see another doctor. It was he who discovered that she was pregnant. When told about the pain under her arm, the doctor was concerned. He sent Heather to a specialist. The specialist, Dr. Williams, discovered that the soreness was caused by a growth. Heather had breast cancer. The specialist said that if Heather had been correctly diagnosed a year ago, the cancer probably could have been successfully treated—but not now. The tumor had grown considerably, and the pregnancy prevented proper treatment.

Dr. Williams recommended that the baby be aborted immediately and that a radical mastectomy (removal of both breasts) be performed at once, followed by radiation and chemotherapy.

Heather was devastated. She wanted a second opinion. Two days and three medical opinions later, the prognosis was exactly the same: Abort the baby and have the surgery.

Heather and Jerry talked over the options very carefully. Jerry wanted Heather to abort the baby and follow the doctors' instructions. Heather wanted to have the baby. Jerry reluctantly agreed to go along with Heather. The doctors were furious. Surgery and radiation treatments could seriously harm the baby. "Then I won't have the radiation treatment," Heather said. "I won't have the surgery either. The baby is too important to me." She decided to wait until after the baby was born before having her cancer treated. All the doctors, Heather's family, her husband, *everyone*, disagreed with her decision, but Heather wanted her baby, and she would not allow it to be aborted.

Six months later, Heather's baby was born. Unfortunately, the baby was born with a serious birth defect, possibly caused by the antibiotics that Heather had taken early in her pregnancy. After recuperating from the birth of her baby, Heather had the surgery and the therapy. She gave up her job to stay home with her baby.

Jerry never did accept the new baby. He could not forgive Heather for risking her life and possibly leaving him with a child to raise alone. Eventually, he moved out and filed for divorce.

Heather's cancer is now in remission but the doctors cannot say when or if it will return.

▶ Rank the following characters from best to worst: Heather, Jerry, Dr. Hadley, Dr. Williams.

▶ Provide a reason for each of the rankings.

● Scripture Guide:    Psalm 139:13–15        Philippians 3:13–14
                      John 16:33             1 Thessalonians 5:18
                      Romans 8:28–29

# 64 ■ THE LAST TO KNOW

Ever since Lee overheard his parents talking about Skip's parents, he had been dying to find out if what they said was true. "Hey, Skip, my folks said your parents had to get married because your mom was pregnant with you. That's not true, is it?" Lee could tell by the look on Skip's face that he never should have said anything. Skip didn't reply. He didn't have to. It was obvious that he knew nothing.

When Skip got home, he stormed downstairs to confront his mother. "Mom, did you and Dad have to get married? Were you pregnant with me? I want to know the truth, Mom."

Lana felt she had no choice. She and her husband, Rob, had discussed this many times. Rob did not believe Skip should ever know. Lana disagreed and could not keep quiet any longer. "Skip, I've wanted to tell you for a long time, but your fath—but we just didn't know how or when to tell you. Yes, it's true."

Skip did not respond. He just sat there, looking out the window. Finally, he said, "Mom, have you and Dad been talking about getting a divorce?"

Lana was caught off-guard again. "Well, Skip, we have been talking about it, yes."

Skip stood up. "I thought so. I knew you and Dad were unhappy. Now I know why. It's me. You should have never gotten married!" Skip said he wanted to be alone and went to his room.

Lana didn't know what to do. She was afraid to tell Rob, but knew she must. When Rob came home, she told him what happened. He exploded with anger. "How could you do that? Now you've made it impossible for me to have any kind of relationship with him. I'll never be able to look him in the eye! Didn't you stop to think what this would do to Skip? Why couldn't you have denied it?"

Rob went up to Skip's room. He knocked on the door. There was no answer. Rob went inside. The room was very neat, but Skip was gone. All Rob found was a note. Skip had run away from home.

Rank the following characters from best to worst: Skip, Lana, Rob, Lee, Lee's parents.

 Provide a reason for each of the rankings.

 Scripture Guide:    Acts 24:16         Galatians 6:7
                          Romans 12:9     Philippians 3:13–14
                          2 Corinthians 12:14

# 65 ■ NO PLACE TO GO

Fourteen-year-old Julie had no place to go. Her father had been having a sexual relationship with her since she was nine. At first, she was frightened, but her father said he loved her and that it was normal for a father to express his love. She loved him too and didn't want to hurt him. As Julie got older, though, she realized that something was wrong—very wrong. Her father had warned her not to tell anyone, and she hadn't, but she couldn't keep it to herself any longer. Julie felt guilty that she hadn't stopped this a long time ago. Obviously, she must be partly to blame.

Something else bothered her as well. There were a number of times, as Julie's father had been leaving her room, that Julie's mother had seen him. Her mother had never said anything. Julie wondered if her mom knew.

Julie decided to talk to her minister. She pleaded with him to keep what she said in strictest confidence. Rev. McKirdy promised not to tell a soul. Julie nervously told him her problem. She was not prepared for his response. Rev. McKirdy did not believe her. He tried to suggest that maybe Julie was fantasizing or that maybe she misunderstood what her father was doing. Rev. McKirdy reminded Julie that her father was a deacon in the church and a very devout man of God. He told Julie to pray.

It was a difficult decision, but Julie decided to tell her boyfriend. She believed Mike would understand. Mike looked at her with disgust. "Come on, Julie, with your father? This has been going on for five years? That makes me sick. Why didn't you tell somebody? Why didn't you do something about it before now?" Julie could tell that Mike was genuinely shaken up. When she didn't hear from him for the next few days, she knew their relationship was finished. Julie really felt alone now. She had to do something. She decided to risk talking to her mother.

Julie waited until her father had left for work and then asked her mom to sit down. Julie forced the truth out. Her mother flew into a rage; she was yelling and crying and threatening all at the same time. She told Julie never to bring up the subject again. She told Julie she was wrong to accuse her father of such a horrible act. Julie was crushed. She believed that her mother had known the truth all along but was afraid to admit it.

Julie felt bitter, alone, and depressed. She went to the medicine cabinet and took out her mother's bottle of sleeping pills. She locked her bedroom door and swallowed the entire bottleful. As Julie became more and more drowsy, she kept asking herself why no one had been willing or able to help her.

▶ Who was most responsible for Julie's suicide?

▶ Rank the characters in order from most responsible to least responsible: Mrs. Donaldson, Mr. Donaldson, Julie, Mike, Rev. McKirdy.

▶ Provide a reason for each of the rankings.

● Scripture Guide:  Leviticus 18:6–12     Romans 8:35–39
                    John 15:12            Romans 15:1

# 66 ■ STEPWITCH

"Marci, I want that room cleaned up before you go, or you'll be grounded again. Is that clear?"

Marci's stepmother was at it again. Sometimes Marci felt as though she hated her. She was always yelling at Marci about something. If it wasn't her room, it was her hair or her make-up (too much, of course) or her bathroom ("hang up your towel!") or the stereo (too loud). Marci really couldn't understand what her dad saw in this . . . witch!

When Marci first asked her father if she could go live with her real mom, her father had said she was overreacting. "Look, Marci," he had said, "Jan has treated you very well. She's just asking you to clean up after yourself and abide by some rules. Any mother would expect the same thing." Marci didn't agree. She knew lots of girls who didn't have to clean up their rooms or dress a certain way. It was stupid.

Marci had talked to her real mom about the problem. "Well, Marci," her mother said, "now you know why I divorced your father. Of course he defends her. He always defends what he likes and what he wants. You will never be treated fairly by him. Just look what he did to me." Marci was sorry she brought the subject up. Her mother had been an alcoholic for years. Her father had tried and tried to help her stop drinking *and* carousing. *She* was the one who asked for the divorce, and she didn't even want custody of Marci.

Marci was old enough now to decide if she wanted to live with her real mom, but she loved her dad very much. Marci decided to tell her father that she was thinking about living with her mother. "You can, Marci, if that's what you really want. I can't stop you. I do want you to understand one thing. Once you move, that's it. You can't move in with your mother for a month, decide you don't like the arrangement, and then move back with us."

Marci tried to talk with her stepmother once more to see if they could work things out. Jan responded, "Marci, I am not trying to make your life miserable. I love you as if you were my own daughter. I understand how difficult it must be to have a stepmother and to do things the way I want them done, but if you decide to stay here, I will expect you to live by the rules."

That made Marci very angry. How could Jan understand? *Jan doesn't know what it is like to have two mothers, Marci thought, and she sure doesn't know what it was like before Dad remarried. Before Jan came along, it was just him and me. He never cared whether I cleaned up my room. We got along great until the stepwitch arrived.* Marci made up her mind. She was going to live with her real mom.

▶ Rank the following characters from best to worst: Marci, Jan, Marci's dad, Marci's real mom

▶ Provide a reason for each of the rankings.

● Scripture Guide:   Exodus 20:12        Proverbs 30:17
                      Proverbs 19:18      Matthew 19:9
                      Proverbs 20:7

# 67 ■ LOUD AND CLEAR

Miles would never forget this Christmas. It seemed like every year his parents managed to surprise him. This year it was with a stereo. One hundred watts of power, two speakers, tape deck—it was unbelievable. What made it even more surprising was that for the last few months Miles and his folks fought constantly about the volume of his portable radio, which was always on in Mile's room when he was home. "You will notice," his parents said, "that this stereo includes a very nice set of earphones. We hope that when we are in the house, you will use them."

In just six short months, war had broken out. Mile's grandmother had become too sick to live alone and had moved in. She couldn't stand any noise at all, let alone a stereo. Each morning the same thing would happen. Miles would get up for school, turn the stereo up, and keep it on until he went upstairs for breakfast. While he was taking a shower, his grandmother would complain, and Miles' parents would walk into his room and turn off his stereo. Miles would then return from his shower and turn the stereo back on. No one said a word, but the same ritual went on every morning. Then, one day after school, Miles walked into his room, and his stereo was gone.

When Mile's parents came in, he knew what had happened. "Miles," his father said, "I am sorry, but your mother and I have sold your stereo." That was all they could say before Miles walked out. He was so angry he didn't know what he was going to do. He stomped out of the house, slammed the door, and headed straight for . . . he didn't know where. He couldn't understand how his folks could do this to him. It was *his* stereo. How could his own parents give him something and then take it back? He stayed out as long as he could.

When he finally came home his parents were waiting for him. "Miles," his father said, "I'm really disappointed in you. We gave you the stereo with the hope that you would use it wisely. For the past six months, we have continually asked you to respect our wishes and your grandmother's wishes to keep the volume down. You've ignored us. We even asked Rev. Peterson what to do, and he agreed that if you weren't willing to abide by our wishes, then we would be justified in taking the stereo. So that's what we have done."

Miles pleaded, "But why didn't you at least warn me that you were going to take it away if I didn't do better. I don't think you have been fair at all!"

His dad looked at Miles. "Miles, we warned you repeatedly that we would have to take drastic action, and you chose to ignore us. We think someday you will understand that being able to listen to your music at full volume is not the most important thing in your life."

Miles just looked at them coldly and thought to himself, *It may not be important to you or the minister, but it is important to me. If that's the way things are going to be around here, then maybe I won't worry about what's important to you!*

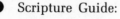 Rank the following characters from best to worst: Miles, Miles' parents, Rev. Peterson, Miles' grandmother.

▶ Provide a reason for each of the rankings.

● Scripture Guide:     Proverbs 4:1–4          Ephesians 4:26
                       Luke 6:30–31

# 68 ■ THE DUD YOUTHWORKER

Everyone in the youth group at First Church was stunned. Skip had been their youth director for the last three years. He was tall, good-looking, super funny, and a great athlete. The attendance at the youth group had grown from seventeen to about seventy. Sometimes, at special meetings, there were as many as two hundred. There was always something neat going on—ski trips, water-ski weekends, summer and winter camps. Now Skip was leaving to go to seminary. Why couldn't he stay at First Church? Skip said that it had been a tough decision, but his wife wanted to start having a family, and Skip needed to get his education out of the way. It was impossible to raise a family on a youth director's salary. The church, he said, would make sure the youth program continued just like it was now. The whole thing blew over because Skip wasn't leaving right away, and he assured the group that the new youth director would be great.

Then Charles showed up. The Rev. Charles G. Wonderly. He was overweight, just out of seminary, and not very good looking. And he was no fun. None of the youth group was impressed. There were so many "Charles" jokes floating around that no one could even say his name with a straight face.

"This is ridiculous," Ken, a leader of the group, complained, "there won't be any kids left in our youth group if we don't get rid of this nerd." The kids tried to call Skip, but he had already moved and hadn't even left a number where he could be reached. In some ways, the kids felt abandoned by Skip and began to wonder just how much he cared about them.

The leaders of the youth group went to the pastor. They tried to get their minister to understand that the youth program was going to disintegrate unless they got rid of Charles. The minister said that he understood their concern but had full confidence in Charles. The kids left the meeting frustrated. They decided to give Charles three more weeks, and if things didn't get better, they would tell their parents they were finished with the youth group until Charles left.

Everyone agreed with that except Teresa. Teresa was a loner, a rather homely girl who never liked Skip and his fancy programs. She also resented the kids who never paid attention to her. Teresa said that the kids shouldn't be going to the youth group because of the youth director; they should be going to learn about God. She tried to convince everyone that even if Charles wasn't as cool as Skip, maybe he knew God better than Skip did. The rest of the group disagreed. They pointed out that if no kids wanted to come, than there wouldn't be anyone in the youth group to learn about God.

Charles did *not* get any better, and eventually, a lot of the kids quit coming. Teresa continued to attend First Church. Suddenly, just six months after he had become the youth director, Charles quit to take a pastorate at a small church. When he quit there were only seven kids attending the youth group, and they only met twice a month. The youth group was in shambles, and Teresa was very disillusioned.

▶ Rank the following characters in the story from best to worst: Skip, Skip's wife, Ken, Teresa, the minister, Charles.

▶ Provide a reason for each of the rankings.

 Scripture Guide:     Matthew 28:20        1 Corinthians 11:18
                     1 Corinthians 1:10–13   1 Peter 3:8

# 69 ■ NOBODY WILL KNOW

How could she be pregnant? Tess had broken up with Don a month ago, and they had only made that one mistake. What a mistake it was turning out to be!

Tess was a very devout Christian. She was active in her youth group and was deeply committed to her faith. So were her parents, Mr. and Mrs. Connell. Her parents had warned her. Gary, her youth director, had warned her. It seemed like everyone had warned her. Tess had prayed really hard that she would not get pregnant. She had asked for forgiveness and had immediately broken off her relationship with Don. But apparently, all her praying didn't matter.

Tess decided to confide in her best friend, Jennifer. Jennifer told Tess to get an abortion. "Your parents will never know, Tess. No one will know." Tess did not believe in abortion, but if she had this baby it would ruin her life, her parents' lives, Don's life, and . . . well, the consequences would just be disastrous. Jennifer encouraged her, "Tess, it's the only way. It's easy, and no one gets hurt." Tess decided to go ahead with the abortion.

"What's this?" Mrs. Connell was standing over Tess. Mr. Connell was right behind. Mrs. Connell was holding a business card from the Youth Care Pregnancy Counseling Center. "Tess, are you pregnant? What is going on?"

Tess was very frightened. "Where did you get that, Mom? Did you go rummaging through my purse again?"

"It doesn't matter where or how I got this, Tess. I want to know what is going on."

"Okay, Mother, okay. No, I'm not pregnant, but I did get an abortion. I'm okay, so don't worry."

Tess's mother was shocked. "Don't worry! My daughter gets pregnant, has an abortion, and I'm not supposed to worry?" Tess was very confused, and her mother's continuous barrage of questions was making her even more confused. Her father just stared at her. She could tell he was hurt and disappointed.

Tess couldn't hold it back any longer. She thought she could get through it alone, but now she realized she couldn't. Tess looked at her mother and father. "Mom and Dad, I lied. I mean, I *am* pregnant, but I didn't get an abortion. I was going to—that's why I have the business card—but I haven't gone yet."

She was not prepared for her parents' response. "What! You mean you didn't get an abortion? You mean you are still pregnant? Now what will we do?"

Tess's new revelation did quiet her parents down, but she could tell they were not pleased. The conversation they were now having was even more revealing. Her parents sat there talking as though she wasn't even present. They were discussing all the options, *including* abortion. Tess was horrified that her parents could actually consider her getting an abortion when they had always taught her it was wrong.

Finally, they looked at Tess and said, "Tess, based on the fact that you are so young, and there is so much at stake, we think you should go ahead with the abortion, but only if it is done by a recognized doctor."

Tess could not believe what she was hearing. Her parents were suggesting an abortion. "So," Tess said bitterly, "abortion is wrong for everyone else, I guess, unless it's your own daughter?"

Mrs. Connell spoke softly now, "That's not true, Tess. We still believe abortion is wrong, but sometimes there can be things more wrong than abortion."

Tess stood up. "Yeah, Mom, I see what you mean. What is more wrong than abortion is having your friends find out that your wonderful Christian daughter is pregnant. That's what's really wrong, isn't it?"

▶ Rank the following characters from best to worst: Tess, Don, Jennifer, Mr. Connell, Mrs. Connell.

▶ Provide a reason for each of the rankings.

 Scripture Guide:   Romans 8:28–29     Philippians 3:13–14
                                2 Corinthians 12:14  Colossians 3:1–3
                                Ephesians 5:16–17

# 70 ■ DOUBLE CROSS

Laura and her boyfriend, Al, had been hassling over whether or not to have sex. Laura thought intercourse before marriage was wrong. Al didn't. Laura's best friend, Sally, and her boyfriend, Bob, had been having intercourse for over a year. Sally told Laura she was crazy not to do it with Al. Al gave Laura an ultimatum. He suggested that if Laura would not have sex with him, then she must not love him. Laura still said no, so Al broke up with her.

Laura was very upset about Al breaking up with her. One night while out at a shopping center, Laura ran into Bob, Sally's boyfriend. Bob seemed very concerned about her, so Laura agreed to go out for a soda and to talk. Bob was very understanding and before Laura knew what was happening, she and Bob were kissing. Laura knew she shouldn't do this, but it felt so good to be with Bob now that Al had left her. Somehow they ended up at the beach and before the night was over, they had sex.

Laura didn't hear from Bob again, but about a week after the beach incident, Sally came to Laura devastated. She confided she had herpes and that she got it from Bob. "Did you know that Bob was sleeping around with a bunch of other girls?" Sally asked.

Laura tried not to worry. She had had sex with Bob only once, but she noticed that she had some sores on her genital area. She was frightened and decided to tell Sally about her one night with Bob. Sally just looked at Laura with disgust and started laughing, "So, you *did* have sex with Bob? I thought so. Some friend you are. Well, Laura, you can find someone else's shoulder to cry on. I *don't* have herpes. I just wanted to see who Bob was playing around with. Now I know. Thanks for being such a good Christian friend."

Sally then confronted Bob, who told Sally that everything had been Laura's fault. "Hey, she came on to me. I just couldn't help it. She got me all turned on and said it would really hurt her if I didn't. Honest."

When Al heard about Laura and Bob, he called Laura up and told her he would like to get back together. Laura agreed to go steady again.

▶ Rank the following characters in the story from best to worst: Laura, Al, Sally, Bob.

▶ Provide a reason for each of the rankings.

● Scripture Guide:    Proverbs 17:17        1 Thessalonians 4:3
                      1 Corinthians 13:4–7   James 1:22
                      Galatians 6:7–8

# 71 ■ DOUBLE DATE—DOUBLE TROUBLE

Mark and Trevor, both juniors in high school, decide to go on a double date. Mark invites his girl friend, Julie, and Trevor invites his girl friend, Kim. Mark has just acquired his driver's license. The night of the double date is the first time he has been allowed to take the family car. Mark's father tells him there are only two rules: Be home on time, and do not drive out of town.

Mark gets home from his date and says that everything went great. Mark's dad asks how Kim, who lives forty miles out of town, got home. Mark tells him that Trevor's parents took her home.

The next day, Mark and his father attend a high-school basketball game together. Mark's dad sees Trevor and comments that he looks a little glum. Mark says that Trevor is on restriction because he went out with Kim last night. It seems that Trevor has been restricted from dating Kim but went out with her anyway, without his parents' knowledge. Mark's dad thinks for a minute and then says, "But, Mark, if Trevor took Kim out last night without his parents' knowledge, then who took Kim home?" Mark starts to say that Kim's parents came in town and picked her up, but realizes, in the middle of his sentence, that he's been caught. Mark's dad says, "You took Kim home, didn't you? You not only disobeyed my request that you not go out of town, but you lied to me, right?"

Mark looked a little pale, "Yes, Dad."

"You are on restriction, Mark, indefinitely! I just don't understand how you could lie to me the first time you are allowed to use the car."

Mark's explanation is as follows: He didn't know that Trevor was restricted from dating Kim until he met them for the date, and he did not know he had to take her home until then, either. Trevor apologized to Mark and promised to pay for all Mark's gas for the evening. Trevor said that they wouldn't have to worry about getting caught.

Mark's dad said that all Mark had to do was to call him and tell him the situation. He said that, chances were, he would have understood and allowed Mark to drive Kim home or would have taken her home himself.

▶ Rank the following characters by who was most responsible for Mark's restriction: Mark, Trevor, Kim, Julie, Mark's father.

▶ Provide a reason for each of the rankings.

 Scripture Guide:     Psalm 1:1–6          Proverbs 20:17
                      Psalm 15:1–2         James 3:13–18

# 72 ■ LITTLE THINGS MEAN A LOT

John and Linda were very active in their youth group. Their best friends were Ken and Sue. Ken was one of the leaders of the youth group. The two couples spent most of their weekends together at church activities or at school events.

During Christmas vacation, John, Linda, Ken, and Sue attended the church high-school retreat. The speaker in the conference spoke about living the Christian life in all areas. He pointed out that seemingly little things such as lying, cheating, and disobeying your parents were important. At the end of the conference, Linda, Ken, and Sue rededicated their lives to Christ. John did not. He was not sure about Christianity anymore. He wanted to know why God didn't keep his parents from getting a divorce. His parents were Christians and God didn't do anything to stop their divorce, even though John prayed.

After they came back from camp, John and Linda started having tension in their relationship. Linda didn't want to write John's English papers any longer. She wouldn't let him look at her answers during the algebra exam. John became angry. He thought Linda was being ridiculous, and he got Ken and Sue to agree with him. They all talked to Linda after school one day. They pointed out that they were all Christians, that Linda and John were practically married, that they didn't take drugs or drink, and that Linda shouldn't get upset about things that didn't matter.

Linda was hurt. She was angry with John for turning Ken and Sue against her. After thinking about it for a day, she broke up with John. That weekend John went out and got drunk with a bunch of friends. He told them that Linda was a religious phony and a sleaze.

When Linda heard about what John had said, she was very upset. She went to her youth director and asked him if she had done the right thing. The youth director encouraged Linda by telling her that she was being a good witness and that John and her friends would be impressed with her commitment. In the long run, he thought, they would respect her. She could count on her Christian friends to be there for support.

That night, when Linda attended youth group, Ken and Sue wouldn't talk to her. Linda began to wonder if what her youth director had said was really true.

▶ Rank the following characters from best to worst: Linda, John, Ken, Sue, the youth director.

▶ Provide a reason for each of the rankings.

 Scripture Guide:    Deuteronomy 13:6−8    Proverbs 17:17
Psalm 41:1    Hebrews 10:23−25

# 73 ■ THE CHAMPAGNE DINNER

Kirk and Chris have been going together for over a year. Kirk is a senior in high school and Chris is a junior. Both of them are involved in the youth group at their church. Recently, Kirk found out that his parents were going to get a divorce. Since then, Kirk has been very upset. As a result, he and Chris have become more sexually intimate. Chris has resisted actual intercourse because she feels that Christians should wait. However, because Kirk has been so torn up over his parents, she has been finding it harder and harder to say no.

Harold and Denise are Kirk and Chris's best friends. They, too, have been going together for over a year. They are also very active in the youth group. They have attended many camps and retreats together, have decided they are going to be married, and believe God is in their relationship. Harold and Denise have a very active sex life, and they see no contradiction between their sexual involvement and their Christian faith. After all, they are both Christians, they take precautions, and they plan on getting married.

During Easter break, Kirk, Chris, Harold, and Denise spent the day at the beach. At the end of the day, as they drive home, they decide to stop at a restaurant. They have such a good time at dinner that Kirk suggests buying some champagne and having a little celebration. Chris is reluctant, but the rest of them argue that if they get just one bottle they won't get drunk.

After dropping Harold and Denise off, Kirk invites Chris into his house. His parents are gone for the weekend. Chris agrees. Before the night is over, Kirk and Chris have sexual intercourse.

The next day Chris feels terribly guilty. She feels like she has let down God, her parents, and everyone. She also feels like a hypocrite. She confides all these feelings to Denise, but Denise doesn't understand. After all, Denise reasons, Chris loves Kirk, and they are both Christians. Kirk is hurting right now, and Chris is giving him what he needs.

Chris doesn't feel any better. She calls her youth director who agrees to see her the next day. They meet, and he explains that Chris has not committed the unpardonable sin, nor is she a hypocrite. He says God can forgive her. He also points out that even though she is sorry and asks God to forgive her, her relationship with Kirk will be more difficult because it will be hard to keep from having sex again. He adds that although Kirk is going through a rough time, sex is not the way to deal with the problem.

Chris breaks up with Kirk, even though she still cares a lot for him.

▶ Rank the following characters from best to worst: Kirk, Chris, Denise, Harold, the youth director.

▶ Provide a reason for each of the rankings.

● Scripture Guide:     John 8:11          Philippians 2:12–16
                        1 Corinthians 6:18–20   1 John 2:15–17

# 74 ■ THE SENIOR PROM

Stephanie and Darlene have talked about the Senior Prom since they were in junior high school. They used to stay up until all hours of the night discussing what kind of dress each of them would wear and who they wanted to go with. Who would have thought that their dreams would be ruined?

Four years later, Stephanie and Darlene were both seniors. They were going to the prom with their boyfriends, Cliff and Roger, two very popular guys who were leaders in the Neighborhood Church youth group. Stephanie and Darlene were very active as well, and both girls' parents were very religious.

Neighborhood's youth group was very large and active. Everyone thought that the youth director, Tim, was a really neat guy—until the unthinkable happened. Tim announced that the church would be sponsoring a big all-night party and dinner *as an alternative to the prom*. Of course, it would be held on the same night as the prom.

When Tim found out that Stephanie, Darlene, Roger, and Cliff were all going to the prom, he asked them to stay after the youth-group meeting and talk about it. He told them that he didn't think going to the prom was a good witness for Christ. There would be a lot of drinking, and as leaders in the group, they needed to set an example. All four of them told Tim they were sorry, but they were still going to the prom. It was only four weeks away, the girls had already purchased their dresses, and the guys had reserved their tuxedos. They explained that they wouldn't be drinking and didn't see anything wrong with dancing—especially at a prom, wearing formals and tuxes. Tim pointed out that none of their objections were a problem. They could even wear their dresses and tuxes. However, all agreed they still would not attend the church activity. End of crisis—or so everyone thought—until they got home.

Both Stephanie and Darlene's parents knew about the alternative to the prom. Tim had contacted them earlier that day and asked them to chaperone the church activity. (He called *before* he knew that Stephanie and Darlene would not be coming.) The girls' parents told them they would have to go to the church activity and *not* the prom. They said that it wouldn't be fair to Tim or to the church or to the youth group if they, as leaders of the youth group, didn't support the church. They added it would be very embarrassing for them to chaperone an event their own children didn't attend. No matter how much Stephanie and Darlene protested, their parents said they could not go to the prom.

When Stephanie told Cliff, he refused to go to the church event, and he said that if Steph couldn't go to the prom, then he would take someone else. When Darlene told Roger, it was a different story. Roger broke up with Darlene. Roger said he was tired of the youth group and tired of her parents always saying no to things that were fun and harmless. Darlene ended up not going to the prom or the church event. Stephanie told her parents she was going to the church event but went to the prom with Cliff instead. She was put on restriction for a month, but she thought it was worth it.

▶ Rank the following characters from best to worst: Stephanie, Darlene, Roger, Cliff, Stephanie's parents, Darlene's parents, Tim.

▶ Provide a reason for each of the rankings.

 Scripture Guide:   Proverbs 1:8        Ephesians 6:1–4
                    1 Corinthians 8:9   Colossians 3:20–21
                    Galatians 5:13

# 75 ■ WHO KILLED RAOUL?

Raoul was a tough kid. You had to be to survive in Haiti. This past year had been a nightmare for him. He and his parents had been one of the luckier families in Haiti. They owned a small piece of land that they were able to farm. It was hard work, but they were always able to provide enough food for their family and still have some left over for other families. Most months, they were even able to save a little money.

Then the nightmare started. The government condemned their land. Government troops showed up late one night and demanded that they abandon their property because the government had sold it to a large U.S.-owned corporation. Raoul's parents refused, and they told the government troops to leave. Then they met with all the other landowners and suggested that they form a protest movement.

Two weeks later, Raoul's sister disappeared. Raoul's family knew they would never see her again. Just one week later, Raoul's brother was found beaten so severely that his brain was damaged.

Raoul's family broke. They decided to leave Haiti and try to find freedom from oppression. They collected all their savings and purchased passage on a small illegal boat to America. The boat was too small and too crowded and was guarded by three men with submachine guns. After they put out to sea, the gunmen took everyone's wallets, money, jewelry, and anything else that had value. Then the storm came. Only ten of the thirty-three people survived. Raoul was one of them.

When Raoul regained consciousness, he was in an American detention camp. It was there that he learned about a large Haitian community in New York. Raoul and several others escaped from the camp one night and made it to New York City. They talked a Haitian cab driver into taking them to the Haitian part of town.

Raoul found a family to stay with for a while, but when it became obvious that he couldn't find a job, the family asked him to leave. He began to roam the streets and soon met up with a small gang of Haitians who survived by committing muggings and small-time robberies. It wasn't long before he saw his participation with the gang as a way to survive and to eventually get out of New York and establish himself as a potential citizen.

After Raoul participated in a few muggings, he began to like what he was doing. It was easy, and there was little risk of being caught. Then Paulo, the gang leader, asked Raoul if he would like to become part of a select group and participate in much more "important" activities—like robbing banks. At first Raoul refused, but then he realized that if his share of the money was enough, he could get out of New York and make a legitimate start. He decided to participate in the robbery of a jewelry store.

The night of the robbery something went wrong. A silent alarm was tripped. When the gang came out of the store, the police were waiting. The gang members began to run. Paulo pulled out a gun and shot at the officers. The police shot back. Raoul was killed.

▶ Rank the following characters on the basis of who was most responsible for Raoul's death? Raoul, the Haitian government, Raoul's parents, Paulo, the U.S. Corporation that purchased Haitian property, the officials at the detention camp.

▶ Provide a reason for each of the rankings.

 Scripture Guide:    2 Chronicles 21:8–20    Micah 6:9–16
                     Proverbs 14:31         Matthew 26:11
                     Ecclesiastes 5:8–9

129

# 76 ■ CHOOSING BETWEEN MOM AND DAD

Belinda's parents' divorce was final. No one except Belinda and her parents knew the real reason why the divorce had occurred. Belinda's dad was a homosexual. Belinda felt sorry for her mom because she had been humiliated, embarrassed, and deeply depressed over the whole thing.

Belinda had decided to stay with her mom after the divorce. Her dad *did* seem genuinely sorry for what had happened, and most important to Belinda, he told her that he still loved her very much. He had written Belinda a beautiful letter in which he apologized for hurting both Belinda and her mother. In the letter, her father described his battle with homosexuality—a battle that had been going on since he was a little boy. He shared that he had tried therapy and had sought help from a number of ministers, but nothing had worked. Finally, he came to the conclusion that he could no longer fight his homosexuality.

Belinda still loved her father, and his letter only made her love him more. She wanted to talk with him and be with him, but she knew if she did, her mother would be deeply hurt. Even the mention of her father's name made her mother become hysterical.

Belinda was torn between her father and mother but decided it was better for both of them if she stayed with her mother and had limited contact with her father. She knew her father would be hurt too, but she thought he could handle the hurt better.

One afternoon, about two months after the divorce, Belinda went with a friend to a local shopping center. Her friend had to use the bathroom, so they both went to a restaurant in the mall. As they walked through the lounge to the bathroom, Belinda saw her mother and a strange man holding hands and talking intimately. She was crushed. All of a sudden, everything was upside down, and nothing made sense anymore.

When Belinda came home she called her father and told him what she had seen. Her father told her that he wasn't surprised. He said he had known about her mother's affair for a long time, but that under the circumstances, he could understand. He encouraged Belinda not to be so harsh on her mother, but Belinda could not get herself to forgive her mother. Maybe her father *was* a homosexual, but at least he wasn't an adulterer.

Belinda made up her mind to go stay with her father. After she packed, Belinda left a note for her mother and then left.

▶ Rank the following characters from best to worst: Belinda, Belinda's mother, Belinda's father.

 Scripture Guide:     Exodus 20:14          1 Corinthians 6:9–11
                      Deuteronomy 6:6–7     1 Corinthians 7:3–4
                      Psalm 103:10–12       Hebrews 13:4
                      Mark 10:9

# 77 ■ A GIFT FROM GOD

Matt prayed quietly at the end of the church service. He had asked God many times to deliver him from his habit. It controlled him—for no matter how much he prayed, it was still there. He was trying hard to live in a right relationship with God, but ... the problem was masturbation. Matt had been masturbating regularly since he was twelve. He was now sixteen. He knew it was wrong, but when he masturbated he felt both good and bad at the same time.

Last week his mother had walked into his bedroom at the wrong time. He wasn't sure whether she knew what he was doing, but the next day he found a book about sex on his bed. He felt guilty about masturbating and very confused after reading the book. The author said that masturbation was a "gift from God," but Matt remembered his church's youth director saying that masturbation was a sin and not God's will. Matt had tried to find something in the Bible related to his problem but couldn't find anything.

Matt had even shared his problem with his best friend, Pete. Pete said that he had masturbated a few times but that he didn't like it. Matt thought about talking to his youth director, but he knew that he would just say to quit doing what he was doing and pray that God would take the desire away.

Matt's older brother advised him to find a girl friend. He said that Matt was just horny and needed a girl.

▶ Rank the following characters from best to worst: Matt, Matt's older brother, Pete, Matt's youth director.

▶ Provide a reason for each of the rankings.

 Scripture Guide:     Psalm 119:44–45     2 Corinthians 3:17
                                     Matthew 5:28        Galatians 5:13
                                     Romans 14:22